THE CENTRAL AMERICANS

Senior Consulting Editor

Senator Daniel Patrick Moynihan

Consulting Editors

Ann Orlov
Managing Editor, Harvard
Encyclopedia of American
Ethnic Groups

M. Mark Stolarik
*President, The Balch Institute
for Ethnic Studies, Philadelphia*

David M. Reimers
*Professor of History,
New York University*

James F. Watts
*Chairman, History Department,
City College of New York*

The Peoples of North America

THE CENTRAL AMERICANS

Faren Bachelis

CHELSEA HOUSE PUBLISHERS
New York   Philadelphia

LINCOLN SCHOOL

On the cover: A Salvadoran mother and child in Washington, D.C.

CHELSEA HOUSE PUBLISHERS
Editor-in-Chief: Nancy Toff
Executive Editor: Remmel T. Nunn
Managing Editor: Karyn Gullen Browne
Copy Chief: Juliann Barbato
Picture Editor: Adrian G. Allen
Art Director: Maria Epes
Manufacturing Manager: Gerald Levine

The Peoples of North America
Senior Editor: Sean Dolan

Staff for THE CENTRAL AMERICANS
Associate Editor: Abigail Meisel
Deputy Copy Chief: Nicole Bowen
Editorial Assistant: Elizabeth Nix
Picture Research: PAR/NYC
Assistant Art Director: Loraine Machlin
Senior Designer: Noreen M. Lamb
Production Manager: Joseph Romano
Cover Illustration: Paul Biniasz
Banner Design: Hrana L. Janto

Copyright © 1990 by Chelsea House Publishers, a division of Main Line Book Co.
All rights reserved. Printed and bound in the United States of America.

First Printing

1   3   5   7   9   8   6   4   2

Library of Congress Cataloging-in-Publication Data
Bachelis, Faren Maree.
   The Central Americans / Faren Bachelis.
      p.   cm. —(Peoples of North America.)
   Bibliography: p.
   Includes index.
   Summary: Discusses the history, culture, and religion of the Central Americans,
factors encouraging their emigration to North America, and their acceptance as an
ethnic group there.
   ISBN 0-87754-868-4
        0-7910-0284-5 (pbk.)
   1. Central American Americans—Juvenile literature.   [1. Central
American Americans.]   I. Title.   II. Series.   89-9905
E184.C34B33   1989   CIP
972.8—dc20   AC

CONTENTS

THE PEOPLES OF NORTH AMERICA

CHELSEA HOUSE PUBLISHERS

A NATION
OF NATIONS

Daniel Patrick Moynihan

The Constitution of the United States begins: "We the People of the United States . . ." Yet, as we know, the United States is not made up of a single group of people. It is made up of many peoples. Immigrants from Europe, Asia, Africa, and Central and South America settled in North America seeking a new life filled with opportunities unavailable in their homeland. Coming from many nations, they forged one nation and made it their own. More than 100 years ago, Walt Whitman expressed this perception of America as a melting pot: "Here is not merely a nation, but a teeming Nation of nations."

Although the ingenuity and acts of courage of these immigrants, our ancestors, shaped the North American way of life, we sometimes take their contributions for granted. This fine series, *The Peoples of North America*, examines the experiences and contributions of the immigrants and how these contributions determined the future of the United States and Canada.

Immigrants did not abandon their ethnic traditions when they reached the shores of North America. Each ethnic group had its own customs and traditions, and each brought different experiences, accomplishments, skills, values, styles of dress, and tastes in food that lingered long after its arrival. Yet this profusion of differences created a singularity, or bond, among the immigrants.

The United States and Canada are unusual in this respect. Whereas religious and ethnic differences have sparked intolerance throughout the rest of the world—from the 17th-century religious wars to the 19th-century nationalist movements in Europe to the near extermination of the Jewish people under Nazi Germany— North Americans have struggled to learn how to respect each other's differences and live in harmony.

Millions of immigrants from scores of homelands brought diversity to our continent. In a mass migration, some 12 million immigrants passed through the waiting rooms of New York's Ellis Island; thousands more came to the West Coast. At first, these immigrants were welcomed because labor was needed to meet the demands of the Industrial Age. Soon, however, the new immigrants faced the prejudice of earlier immigrants who saw them as a burden on the economy. Legislation was passed to limit immigration. The Chinese Exclusion Act of 1882 was among the first laws closing the doors to the promise of America. The Japanese were also effectively excluded by this law. In 1924, Congress set immigration quotas on a country-by-country basis.

Such prejudices might have triggered war, as they did in Europe, but North Americans chose negotiation and compromise instead. This determination to resolve differences peacefully has been the hallmark of the peoples of North America.

The remarkable ability of Americans to live together as one people was seriously threatened by the issue of slavery. It was a symptom of growing intolerance in the world. Thousands of settlers from the British Isles had arrived in the colonies as indentured servants, agreeing to work for a specified number of years on farms or as apprentices in return for passage to America and room and board. When the first Africans arrived in the then-British colonies during the 17th century, some colonists thought that they too should be treated as indentured servants. Eventually, the question of whether the Africans should be viewed as indentured, like the English, or as slaves who could be owned for life, was considered in a Maryland court. The court's calamitous decree held that blacks were slaves bound to lifelong servitude, and so were their children. America went through a time of moral examination and civil war before it finally freed African slaves and their descendants. The principle that all people are created equal had faced its greatest challenge and survived.

Yet the court ruling that set blacks apart from other races fanned flames of discrimination that burned long after slavery was abolished—and that still flicker today. The concept of racism had existed for centuries in countries throughout the world. For instance, when the Manchus conquered China in the 13th century, they decreed that Chinese and Manchus could not intermarry. To impress their superiority on the conquered Chinese, the Manchus ordered all Chinese men to wear their hair in a long braid called a queue.

By the 19th century, some intellectuals took up the banner of racism, citing Charles Darwin. Darwin's scientific studies hypothesized that highly evolved animals were dominant over other animals. Some advocates of this theory applied it to humans, asserting that certain races were more highly evolved than others and thus were superior.

This philosophy served as the basis for a new form of discrimination, not only against nonwhite people but also against various ethnic groups. Asians faced harsh discrimination and were depicted by popular 19th-century newspaper cartoonists as depraved, degenerate, and deficient in intelligence. When the Irish flooded American cities to escape the famine in Ireland, the cartoonists caricatured the typical "Paddy" (a common term for Irish immigrants) as an apelike creature with jutting jaw and sloping forehead.

By the 20th century, racism and ethnic prejudice had given rise to virulent theories of a Northern European master race. When Adolf Hitler came to power in Germany in 1933, he popularized the notion of Aryan supremacy. *Aryan*, a term referring to the Indo-European races, was applied to so-called superior physical characteristics such as blond hair, blue eyes, and delicate facial features. Anyone with darker and heavier features was considered inferior. Buttressed by these theories, the German Nazi state from

1933 to 1945 set out to destroy European Jews, along with Poles, Russians, and other groups considered inferior. It nearly succeeded. Millions of these people were exterminated.

The tragedies brought on by ethnic and racial intolerance throughout the world demonstrate the importance of North America's efforts to create a society free of prejudice and inequality.

A relatively recent example of the New World's desire to resolve ethnic friction nonviolently is the solution the Canadians found to a conflict between two ethnic groups. A long-standing dispute as to whether Canadian culture was properly English or French resurfaced in the mid-1960s, dividing the peoples of the French-speaking Quebec Province from those of the English-speaking provinces. Relations grew tense, then bitter, then violent. The Royal Commission on Bilingualism and Biculturalism was established to study the growing crisis and to propose measures to ease the tensions. As a result of the commission's recommendations, all official documents and statements from the national government's capital at Ottawa are now issued in both French and English, and bilingual education is encouraged.

The year 1980 marked a coming of age for the United States's ethnic heritage. For the first time, the U.S. Census asked people about their ethnic background. Americans chose from more than 100 groups, including French Basque, Spanish Basque, French Canadian, Afro-American, Peruvian, Armenian, Chinese, and Japanese. The ethnic group with the largest response was English (49.6 million). More than 100 million Americans claimed ancestors from the British Isles, which includes England, Ireland, Wales, and Scotland. There were almost as many Germans (49.2 million) as English. The Irish-American population (40.2 million) was third, but the next largest ethnic group, the Afro-Americans, was a distant fourth (21 million). There was a sizable group of French ancestry (13 million), as well as of Italian (12 million). Poles, Dutch, Swedes, Norwegians, and Russians followed. These groups, and other smaller ones, represent the wondrous profusion of ethnic influences in North America.

Canada, too, has learned more about the diversity of its population. Studies conducted during the French/English conflict showed that Canadians were descended from Ukrainians, Germans, Italians, Chinese, Japanese, native Indians, and Eskimos, among others. Canada found it had no ethnic majority, although nearly half of its immigrant population had come from the British Isles. Canada, like the United States, is a land of immigrants for whom mutual tolerance is a matter of reason as well as principle.

The people of North America are the descendants of one of the greatest migrations in history. And that migration is not over. Koreans, Vietnamese, Nicaraguans, Cubans, and many others are heading for the shores of North America in large numbers. This mix of cultures shapes every aspect of our lives. To understand ourselves, we must know something about our diverse ethnic ancestry. Nothing so defines the North American nations as the motto on the Great Seal of the United States: *E Pluribus Unum*— Out of Many, One.

*Guatemalan refugees who have
entered the United States
without proper documentation
pose for a family portrait but
cover their faces to conceal their
identity. Central Americans who
live illegally in the United
States live in constant fear of
arrest by Immigration and
Naturalization Service officers.*

HAVEN FROM THE HOMELAND

The story of Central American immigration to the United States begins in 1820, when U.S. immigration officials recorded the arrival of two Central American émigrés. Throughout the 1800s and the first 6 decades of the 20th century the number of Central Americans who settled in the United States remained under 10,000—a modest number, especially compared to the millions of European and Asian immigrants who poured into the United States during that same period. Family background as well as their small numbers distinguished many of the Central Americans who made their way north at that time from their European and Asian counterparts. Whereas most other immigrants of the time were uneducated peasants, a large percentage of those who emigrated from Central America in the early and mid-1900s belonged to privileged families from Panama and Costa Rica. Central American immigration increased steadily over the next decades. By 1970 approximately 174,000

Central Americans, hailing from each of the region's 7 countries—Guatemala, Belize, Honduras, El Salvador, Nicaragua, Costa Rica, and Panama—lived in the United States. But this number amounted to only a fraction of the flood of refugees from El Salvador, Guatemala, and Nicaragua who sought haven in the United States over the course of the next two decades.

The bloodshed that erupted in that period and sparked the ongoing great wave of Central American immigration had its roots in the region's long, complex history. For thousands of years indigenous Indians hunted and farmed the Central American highlands and lowlands, where they developed highly complex cultures. The Indians' way of life was shattered by the Spanish conquistadores who began colonizing the area in the early 1500s. The Spanish were originally lured to Central America by their greed for gold, but when they found none they turned to growing crops for export, using Indian slave labor. During more than 300 years of occupation, the Spanish imposed their language, culture, and traditions on the Indians.

Although Spanish rule ended in Central America in 1821, many wealthy Spanish families remained and continued to exercise control in Central America. These families maintained their power by forming alliances with dictators and their armies—a pattern that has continued into the late 20th century. Central America's ruling families also found a powerful ally in the United States. Beginning in the mid-19th century, American businesses invested millions of dollars in the region's banana and coffee plantations and in a Central American railroad. As American capital grew, so too did the role of the U.S. government in protecting those investments through extensive financial and military support of the region's dictators.

In the 1970s, Central Americans staged revolutions against many U.S.-supported military regimes. Bloody civil wars raged in Nicaragua and in El Salvador, where more than 60,000 have died and more than 1.2 million have been forced from their homes. In Guatemala, a brutal military government has carried on a campaign

of terror since the 1950s, killing more than 50,000 people and leaving thousands more without land or livelihood. Unable to work or to live safely in their own or in neighboring countries, many Salvadorans, Guatemalans, and Nicaraguans felt they had no choice but to come to the United States.

Most Salvadorans and Guatemalans have settled in Los Angeles, the country's undisputed Central American capital, which is home to an estimated 350,000 Salvadorans and 110,000 Guatemalans. Large numbers also live in San Francisco and other cities, including Houston, Texas; Washington, D.C.; and New York. Whereas Salvadorans and Guatemalans tend to live on the West Coast, Nicaraguans most frequently settle in

Laborers prepare a coffee harvest for shipment on a plantation in El Salvador. Cash crops such as coffee have dominated Central American agriculture since the 1700s.

Even children—such as this Nicaraguan girl—are drawn into the fray between hostile factions in Central America. In the early 1980s, thousands of young people fled Nicaragua rather than be forcibly inducted into the Sandinista army.

the East, largely in Miami, Florida. No matter what their country of origin, the majority of the estimated 1 million Central Americans who have settled in the United States live here without documentation. Some entered the country with visas that have since expired; others slipped across the border illegally. The U.S. government often uses the term *illegal alien* to refer to these individuals. The term is not widely accepted in the Hispanic community, which prefers to call those without documentation *undocumented migrants*.

So many Central Americans are undocumented because few qualify for permanent resident status in the United States. Under current U.S. immigration law, in effect since 1965, priority is given to educated professionals. Few of the peasants of Central America meet the current requirements. The U.S. Immigration and Naturalization Service (INS), the federal bureau charged with regulating immigration, does have special admission quotas for those seeking political sanctuary, but virtually all of the immigrants from Central America have been deemed economic rather than political refugees, meaning that the INS believes that their primary motivation in coming is to seek a higher standard of living, not to escape political repression. Thus most Central Americans have found it virtually impossible to remain legally in the United States.

Because most Central Americans are here without documentation they live in constant fear of being caught by immigration authorities and deported back to their country of origin. Their legal status affects every aspect of their lives, from jobs and housing to medical care and education. Despite this disadvantage, Central Americans have worked hard to create communities for themselves and their children.

They have opened hundreds of businesses around Los Angeles, enrolled their children in American schools, organized advocacy groups, bolstered the congregations of Catholic churches, and lobbied state and federal legislatures on their own behalf.

Many of those Central Americans who originally intended to stay in the United States only temporarily have decided to make their permanent home here, both because they have grown accustomed to life in the United States and because conditions in Central America are still dangerous. The question that remains is whether the U.S. government will change its policy and allow these refugees to stay here legally or whether Central Americans must continue to live in fear of detection and deportation.

The rolling hills of Costa Rica typify the lush landscape of southern Central America.

A LEGACY OF OPPRESSION

The lands known today as Costa Rica, El Salvador, Guatemala, Honduras, and Nicaragua—the five original republics of Central America—have been embroiled in armed conflict since the first Spanish conquistadores, seeking gold and other precious metals, arrived in North America in 1504. As the world powers competed with one another to establish colonial empires over the next four centuries, both Great Britain and the United States joined Spain in attempting to gain control of Central America. The struggle between the Central Americans and their would-be colonial overlords was often bloody.

In part the colonizers coveted Central America because of its strategic location. The region, which is considered part of North America, may be seen as a land bridge connecting the two American continents. Once the Spanish conquistador Vasco Núñez de Balboa reached the Pacific Ocean in 1513 by crossing the Isthmus of Panama, European merchants and traders, eager to reach the Indies, believed Central America might contain the elusive water passage between the Atlantic and the Pacific. They were to be frustrated in that quest, at least until the 20th century, but fortune seekers, adventurers, prospectors, and colonizers from Spain and elsewhere made the difficult journey to the area nonetheless.

Guatemala, the northernmost country in Central America, abuts Mexico, as does Guatemala's neighbor

19

Belize, formerly British Honduras, which won its full independence from Britain in 1981. In the southernmost region of Central America is Panama, which, like Belize, was not traditionally considered a part of Central America until the 20th century. Aided by the United States, which hoped to obtain from a compliant Panamanian government an agreement to build a canal linking the Atlantic and the Pacific, Panama declared its independence from the South American nation of Colombia in 1903.

The east coast of Central America juts out into the Caribbean Sea, a part of the Atlantic Ocean, and the west coast lies on the Pacific Ocean. Today, as the conquistadores had envisioned, Central America serves as the shortest route between these two bodies

Beginning in the mid-1800s the U.S. government envisioned a Central American waterway linking the Atlantic and Pacific oceans. In 1914 this ambition was realized with the completion of the Panama Canal, which stretches 51 miles across the middle of Panama and joins the two seas.

of water. The Panama Canal, a man-made waterway, was completed in 1914. The region's proximity to both the Atlantic and Pacific oceans makes it one of the principal crossroads of the world.

Central America's mountainous inland rivals its long coastline in natural beauty. In the northern highlands of Guatemala, Honduras, El Salvador, and Nicaragua, volcanic mountains rise to a height of 10,000 feet. The fertile earth in this area has proved perfect for growing coffee, fruit, and corn, among other crops. The southern highlands also feature a dramatic landscape marked by valleys and volcanoes. This area has suffered devastation from earthquakes several times, most recently in 1972 when Nicaragua's capital city, Managua, was destroyed and had to be almost completely rebuilt.

The variety of Central America's terrain is matched by the diversity of its people, who numbered about 25 million in 1984. The population includes descendants of native Indians, African slaves, and Spanish colonists. Each group lives in the same general vicinity as did its ancestors. Descendants of the Indians have settled mainly in the highlands, while people of African origin and those of mixed African and Indian blood tend to inhabit the east coast, where ships once delivered slaves from West Africa. People of European descent live throughout Central America, as do *mestizos*, people of mixed European and Indian ancestry. Although many ethnic groups have long made their home in Central America, only one—the Indians—can legitimately claim to be descended from the region's original inhabitants.

Preconquest Central America

Until the arrival of the Spanish in the 16th century, Central America was an Indian land. Most historians believe that the Indians who came to inhabit Central America migrated on foot over a land bridge that once linked Siberia and Alaska, where today a narrow waterway known as the Bering Strait separates Asia and North America. The first of these wayfarers probably reached North America more than 10,000 years ago, and the migratory process probably took place over a period of thousands of years.

By 2000 B.C. these wanderers had drifted south through the Great Plains and Mexico, finally settling in small farming communities scattered throughout the highland region of Central America, where they cultivated maize and other crops. With the development of agriculture came a more rooted, less mobile existence and an end to the need to roam in search of food. Instead, villagers remained in a single region for generations.

They erected permanent dwellings, which they thatched with dried palm leaves. These dwellings sat isolated from each other but were connected by a network of footpaths cleared through the forest.

Over hundreds of years, traditional societies in Central America evolved independently of each other, until those in the north differed greatly from those in the south. Most of southern Central America, including Panama, eastern Nicaragua, and Costa Rica, contained small agricultural villages. The Indians there grew a variety of tuber plants, including yams, sweet manioc, and sweet potatoes, and also hunted and fished to obtain food. All the villagers worked the land, and all held equal rank within their society. Although certain individuals undoubtedly emerged as leaders by force of character, there was no organized hierarchy, and no one was designated to act as chief.

By contrast, inhabitants of northern Central America lived in complex, stratified societies, the most well known of which was that of the Maya. The Maya controlled thousands of miles of territory from El Salvador and Honduras into Guatemala and Belize; their empire reached north to Mexico's Yucatan Peninsula and as far west as the modern Mexican states of Tabasco and Chiapas.

Although Mayan history spans more than 3,000 years (from approximately 1500 B.C. to A.D. 1697) the Maya enjoyed their greatest period of influence, wealth, and creativity between approximately A.D. 300 and A.D. 900. Mayan achievements from this era rank among the most impressive in the history of the Western Hemisphere. Outstanding architects and engineers, the Maya built huge stone temples in the shape of pyramids that rose more than 200 feet above the ground. Their accomplishments in the arts and sciences were equally impressive. The Maya devised a 13-month calendar that was extraordinary in its accuracy and developed a system of hieroglyphics, or

A ruin in Guatemala stands as testament to the architectural and engineering talents of the Maya. Ancient Mayan structures still exist in Mexico, Guatemala, and Honduras and provide scholars with clues about the Maya's rise to glory and mysterious fall from power.

A Guatemalan woman prepares tortillas—Spanish pancakes—by cooking them on an iron pan over hot coals. Descendants of the Maya have retained many practices of native Indian culture but have also adopted traditions of the Spanish.

picture writing, consisting of approximately 800 characters. Linguists failed to fully decipher this written language until the mid-1980s.

Most of the hieroglyphics were found on stone monuments and on pottery, another endeavor in which the Maya excelled. Mayas painted their ceramics with brilliant designs, and they also produced colorful wall frescoes and illustrated codices. But Mayan artists composed only a small percentage of the population. Most of the Maya, whose population in the 8th century was estimated at 14 million, lived in agricultural communities in houses made of sun-dried earth and straw. They grew beans and maize—still the daily fare of many Central Americans.

As of the 1980s, men and women of Mayan blood accounted for about 45 percent of all Guatemalans, and Mayan descendants could be found also in Mexico and Honduras. Some still practice their traditional crafts, utilizing the skill and creativity handed down from their forebears to make pottery, baskets, and rugs that are genuine works of art as well as the cultural inheritance of a great people. Today the Maya's descendants live in a hybrid culture in which traditional Indian ways are combined with the customs of the Spanish, whose arrival in the New World changed Central America forever.

The Spanish Conquest

The Spanish colonization of the Western Hemisphere began in 1492, when Christopher Columbus, a Genoese mariner sponsored by King Ferdinand and Queen Isabella of Spain, sighted the Caribbean island he called San Salvador. (Most historians believe that Columbus landed on what is known today as Watling's Island.) Although Columbus believed until his death in 1506 that he had reached Asia, the voyages of other sailors soon made it apparent that he had discovered a previously unknown continent, but one as rich as Asia was said to be. Columbus's discovery paved the way for Spanish explorers, the conquistadores, who followed him to America in search of gold. The resis-

tance offered by the Indians was no match for Spanish firepower. Muskets and gunpowder gave the conquistadores an enormous technological advantage in battle, and the Indians were equally frightened by the horses the Spanish rode and the fierce mastiffs and hounds they unleashed before them. (Neither dogs nor horses are native to the Americas.) The conquistadores swept through Mexico, Central America, and South America. In 1521, Hernán Cortés toppled the powerful Aztec empire after capturing the emperor Montezuma in battle and razing the Aztec capital city of Tenochtitlán. That same year Gil González Dávila pushed into western Nicaragua. In 1524, Pedro de Alvarado invaded Guatemala and, after several years of continuous fighting, gained control of the land and its people.

An engraving depicts Spanish explorer Pedro de Alvarado with some of his 700 soldiers during a battle with Indians, probably in Guatemala. The Indians lacked firearms of their own, yet they managed to defeat Alvarado and his troops by placing large boulders behind trees at the top of a hill and then cutting the trees so that the rocks hurtled downward, crushing anything in their path.

The conquistadores' treatment of the Indians was far from humane. Hundreds were slaughtered, and most of those who survived the sword were enslaved. With no natural immunity to the diseases the Spaniards brought with them from Europe, thousands of Indians died of illness. Smallpox, measles, and other plagues quickly reduced the native population to a fraction of its original size. In some parts of the Americas—such as central Mexico—the native population declined by as much as 95 percent.

For a while the Indians bravely attempted to fight off the Spanish. In eastern Nicaragua, a hellish, insect-infested region the Europeans dubbed the Mosquito Coast, the Spaniards at first encountered such stubborn resistance from the Carib Indians that they retreated from the area. In El Salvador, native tribes fought the Spanish for 20 years, but they had little chance against the unbridled ferocity and superior weapons of the newcomers. After one of the first battles there, a Spaniard wrote: "[The] destruction we made amongst them was so great that in a short time none were left alive." Historians estimate that after 50 years of conquest, the Indian population of El Salvador had declined from 500,000 to about 75,000. The conquests of Guatemala, where direct descendants of the Maya led uprisings against Spain's rule well into the 1500s, were similarly bloody. Between 1519 and 1610 the Indian population in Guatemala decreased by approximately two-thirds as a result of disease and warfare.

Not surprisingly, the Indians hated the Spanish. They felt particular disgust at the conquistadores' lust for gold. In Panama, Indians reportedly captured Spanish soldiers and poured molten gold down their throats, saying, "Take your fill of gold!" In the end, however, the Spanish found only a modest amount of gold in Central America. The bulk of the wealth they earned there came from exporting crops back to Europe. These cash crops were grown on *haciendas*, vast estates of land appropriated by the Spanish from the Indians. Deprived of their lands, many of the Indians starved to death. Thousands of others were branded, taken in chains as slaves to labor in the fields where

Indians pour molten gold into the mouths of Spanish adventurers in order to exact revenge for the many atrocities the conquistadores inflicted on them.

they had once grown their own maize, cacao, and other crops. Others were put to work mining gold, silver, and tin.

The abuse of the native population by the Spanish outraged Bartolomé de Las Casas, a missionary who recounted the suffering of native Central and South Americans in *The Tears of the Indians*, published in London in 1556. The Spanish bishop wrote that the Indians "suffered as much as possible the tyranny and bondage which the Christians imposed upon them . . . [and were] subjected to so much evil, butchery, cruelty, bondage, and injustice that no human tongue would be able to describe it." Translated into 42 languages during the late 16th and early 17th centuries, *The Tears of the Indians* eventually led the Spanish crown to abolish the forced labor of Indians in 1642. Yet Indian slavery existed in practice in Central America long after it was officially outlawed.

The Spanish tamed the Indians with the cross as well as the sword. Indians who refused to convert to Catholicism were threatened with death. Missionaries imposed the Spanish language and Spanish customs on the native population. The decline of native religion was mirrored in the weakening of the traditional fam-

Spanish troops round up Indians for enslavement in an engraving from the German edition of The Tears of the Indians *by Bartolomé de Las Casas. The missionary's account of Indian suffering moved Spanish monarchs to outlaw Indian slavery in the New World, but native Central Americans continued to toil in inhuman conditions.*

ily structure of the Indians. So many men were lost to disease and warfare that there were too few males to provide for families and protect them. These changes destabilized native society and made it even easier for Spain to consolidate its control over Central America.

The Oligarchs' Ascension

For approximately 300 years the regions that today comprise Guatemala, El Salvador, Nicaragua, Honduras, and Costa Rica constituted a single administrative district—called Guatemala—within Spain's Latin American empire. The Spanish regarded the present-day nation of Guatemala as the most important territory within their domain, and they built a beautiful capital, Antigua, there. In 1773 an earthquake toppled Antigua, which the Spanish rebuilt and renamed Guatemala City. But the Spanish never considered Guatemala City or any of Central America to be as important as their richer colonies of Mexico and Peru. According to historian Walter LaFeber,

> Most of Central America had been the backwater of the Spanish Empire. One and one-quarter million souls inhabited the area when it became independent of Spain in 1822, but half were Indians and most of those lived in isolation and poverty. The relatively few Spaniards dominated the economy and politics.

By the 19th century, Spain's grip on Central America was slipping. War and national turmoil had left Spain economically ruined and politically divided. No longer a great world power, Spain was unable to stifle revolt in its New World colonies. In May 1821, Mexico declared its independence from Spain. Four months later Central America followed suit and joined a new Mexican empire established by the soldier Agustín de Iturbide. But Iturbide's repressive measures incited much opposition, and his overthrow in 1823 left Central America uncertain of its future direction. Looking to the United States as a model, leaders of the clergy, powerful landowners, and colonial politicians convened at Guatemala City and created a confederation of Central American states that included Guatemala, Honduras, Nicaragua, El Salvador, and Costa Rica. On July 1, 1823, the United Provinces of Central America came into being.

Conflict soon erupted between the five provinces. Arguments broke out between liberals, who wanted a strong federation of the five regions, and wealthy conservatives, who advocated greater independence for each province because they feared losing control over their home republic. The strife between these factions caused bloodshed within and among the republics. In Nicaragua, for example, civil war raged between 1826

On September 15, 1821, Salvadoran leaders convened and formally declared their independence from Spain, an event depicted in this historical painting, which today hangs in the National Palace in San Salvador.

and 1829. By 1842, after years of continuous conflict, the conservatives had won the struggle throughout Central America. They dissolved the union, leaving five separate republics.

Within the republics, about one percent of the population, composed of a few wealthy families, controlled virtually all of the land, wealth, and political power. These influential landowners came to be known as *oligarchs*. In many cases the descendants of the Spanish who had owned the haciendas during the colonial period, the oligarchs generally grew one or two cash crops, such as coffee or indigo, or owned gold and silver mines. The great majority of the population of the Central American nations were left landless and without any means to feed themselves and their families. Most Central Americans were forced either to migrate from their homes or to work in semi-slavery for the oligarchs.

The end of Spanish control of Central America offered an opportunity for other world powers to take an economic and political interest in the region. During the first part of the 19th century, Great Britain became the dominant foreign force in Central America. British financiers and banks invested a fortune to build railroads in Guatemala, Honduras, and Costa Rica. The British government often intervened in Central American affairs, and ships from the empire's powerful fleet constantly plied the coastal waters of Honduras, Nicaragua, and Costa Rica. When the Honduran government refused to pay a debt it owed the British, for example, English warships laid siege to a Honduran port until Honduras agreed to reimburse the royal Crown.

American Involvement

In the 1840s the British hold on Central America was challenged by the United States, which had first shown interest in the region during the administration of President James Monroe. Monroe's secretary of state, John Quincy Adams, believed that European powers in the western hemisphere represented a direct threat to the security of the United States. Adams wanted to send a message to all European powers that

both American continents now fell within the domain of the United States, and he persuaded President Monroe to articulate this position in a message to the Congress, now known as the Monroe Doctrine, delivered on December 2, 1823: "The American continents . . . are henceforth not to be considered as subjects for further colonization by any European powers." Although Monroe's address met with support, few who heard it realized that it would gradually become the cornerstone of American foreign policy in Latin America.

U.S. interest in Central America grew after the United States won one-third of Mexico's territory during the Mexican War, which lasted from 1846 to 1848. Fresh from victory in this conflict, the United States turned its attention to Nicaragua, which the southern wing of the Democratic party viewed as possible ground for the expansion of slavery. While the U.S. government engaged in diplomatic sparring with Great Britain over Nicaragua, where both nations sought to build a canal linking the Atlantic and Pacific oceans, U.S. president James Polk tried unsuccessfully to unite the Central American republics to fight England. In 1850 the dispute ended with the signing of the Clayton-Bulwer Treaty, in which the United States and England agreed to cooperate on any canal built in Central America. Although the United States failed to oust England from Central America, it gained international recognition as an important force in the region.

U.S. interference in Nicaragua did not cease with the Clayton-Bulwer Treaty. In 1854, William Walker, an adventurer and self-proclaimed "grey-eyed man of

In 1854 an American steamship ferrying mail between the United States and Central America unloads its cargo in New Grenada, Panama. During the 1850s the U.S. government established a foothold in Central America and encouraged American businesses to follow suit.

William Walker was born in Nashville, Tennessee, in 1824 and received degrees in both law and medicine by age 26. Walker's Nicaraguan fiasco was foreshadowed in 1853, when he tried to colonize Sonora—a region of Mexico bordering California— and declared himself president of the region. American authorities intervened, however, and arrested Walker for violating neutrality laws. No sooner did a judge acquit Walker of the charges than he began making preparations for his Nicaraguan expedition.

destiny," sailed with an army of 57 from San Francisco to Nicaragua, where they joined with rebels in that country to overthrow the government. Walker declared himself president of Nicaragua and received immediate diplomatic recognition from the United States. Opposed by an alliance of the other Central American states, Walker legalized slavery in Nicaragua in 1856 in a bid to win increased support from the American South. The gambit failed, however, and he was driven from power and back to the United States by Nicaraguan patriots. In 1860 he was executed by a firing squad in Honduras after another failed attempt at Central American intervention.

As the century progressed, the United States gained in economic and military strength, and U.S. influence grew in Central America. In the 1870s, U.S. industrialists poured money into Central American mining companies and into coffee and banana plantations. Railroad baron Cornelius Vanderbilt, a financial backer of Walker, had established a steamship line and railroad in Nicaragua as early as 1850 and continued to consolidate his hold on Nicaraguan transportation after the Civil War. By 1914, in neighboring Honduras, American banana companies controlled nearly 1 million acres, most of the fertile land in the country, thus inspiring the term *banana republic*. Between 1847 and 1914 overall U.S. investments in Central America grew from $21 million to $93 million. This trend has continued throughout the 20th century.

The United States protected its considerable investments by repeated military intervention and by supporting those governments, military leaders, and oligarchs pledged to maintaining the status quo. When Guatemala invaded El Salvador in 1885 to expand its influence in the region, the U.S. government promptly dispatched the navy warship USS *Wachusett* to Central American coastal waters in order to protect American property in Guatemala, El Salvador, and Nicaragua. In 1912, President William Taft ordered the U.S. Marines into Nicaragua to stem social unrest following a U.S.-backed coup that overthrew President José Santos Zelaya. The marines remained in Nicaragua until 1933.

An Era of Dictatorships

The United States has intervened in the domestic affairs of every Central American nation, but its impact on emigration has been greatest in Guatemala, El Salvador, and Nicaragua, the three countries that send the most Central Americans to the United States and Canada each year. The 1980s exodus from Nicaragua, for example, can be traced directly to the repressive dictatorship of Nicaraguan National Guard commander Anastasio Somoza, whom the American government helped elevate to Nicaragua's presidency in 1936.

Somoza amassed a fortune of $60 million during his 20 years as Nicaragua's president. He treated the American-trained National Guard as a personal army, unleashing its force against any opposition movement that gathered support in Nicaragua. Even after Somoza's assassination in 1956, his legacy continued. In 1956 he was succeeded by his eldest son, Luis Somoza Debayle, who was in turn followed by longtime Somoza supporter René Schick Gutiérrez. Gutiérrez held office just until the next Somoza, Anastasio, Jr., could graduate from West Point and return to Nicaragua to assume the presidency.

The Somoza dynasty dominated Nicaragua's economic and political life, and despite widespread opposition the family maintained its power by making itself indispensable to the United States. For nearly 40 years the Somozas worked closely with the Central Intelligence Agency (CIA) to subvert democratic movements in Guatemala and Costa Rica. In 1961, Nicaragua allowed the CIA to use it as a staging ground for its failed invasion of Cuba, an escapade known as the Bay of Pigs operation. Finally, in 1979 a revolutionary group broke the Somozas' grip on Nicaragua. The Sandinist National Liberation Front (FSLN), a guerrilla organization named in honor of Augusto César Sandino, who had led the armed opposition to the earlier U.S. occupation, overthrew the Somoza regime and established itself as the nation's new government. The FSLN victory cost Nicaragua between 40,000 and 50,000 lives.

In 1955, Anastasio Somoza posed for this portrait, flanked by two iron bookends cast in the shape of dueling pistols. The bookends were a gift from one of Somoza's American friends.

In the aftermath of the revolution the Sandinistas gained the support of some nations and the opposition of others. Some Latin American countries and European Socialist parties and governments sent economic and political support to the new government, as did Cuba and the Soviet Union and its allies. In contrast the United States opened its doors to Somoza and his followers and funneled military funding to counter-revolutionary groups, known as the *contras*. (*Contra* is the Spanish word for "against.") Most of the contra groups set up camp in Honduras under the auspices of the U.S. government.

Like the Somozas, the rulers of Guatemala kept a tight reign on the country and maintained their control with the help of a secret police force. General Jorge Ubico Castañeda, a contemporary of the elder Anastasio Somoza, seized power in 1931. Ubico worked closely with the United States—Guatemala's main

In August 1983 soldiers roll through the streets of Guatemala City in a tank, maintaining order in the aftermath of a coup d'état that overthrew the government of General Efrain Rios Mont, who ruled Guatemala by decree for 17 months.

trading partner—to restore the country's ravaged economy in the midst of a worldwide economic depression, but the Guatemalan masses derived no benefit from his rule. Many suffered from new vagrancy laws that allowed police to arrest anyone without a job and place him or her in jobs with the government or with coffee and banana growers for slave wages.

Ubico's domestic policies angered many segments of Guatemalan society, particularly the students and young army officers. In 1944, student-led strikes in Guatemala City triggered a national revolution that forced Ubico to step down in favor of Juan José Arévalo, a university professor. The United States watched with growing alarm as first Arévalo and then his successor Jacobo Arbenz Guzmán carried out long-needed economic reforms, including the redistribution of land in the countryside. In 1952, Arbenz began reclaiming land from the U.S.-controlled United Fruit Company and other powerful growers on behalf of Guatemala's peasants, many of whom were starving because they lacked a place to cultivate their staple diet of beans and maize.

Realizing that Arbenz's reforms challenged the U.S. hold on Guatemala, the administration of Dwight D. Eisenhower approved a CIA plan to destabilize the Central American nation's constitutional government. Led by dissident colonel Carlos Castillo Armas, an army trained by the CIA in Honduras and El Salvador took up arms and overthrew the Arbenz government in 1955. Armas jailed the student and peasant leaders who constituted the most vocal opposition to his regime. The army grew even more thorough in silencing dissent in the late 1960s and early 1970s, when it killed an estimated 20,000 citizens suspected of political agitation. The atrocities alienated even the military's most steadfast ally, the United States, which cut off economic aid to the Guatemalan government in 1977. By that point the military had launched a massive counterinsurgency program directed against the trade unionists, clergy, peasants, and professionals who had organized against the government. The ensuing brutality reached its peak between 1981 and 1984, when government troops burned 400 Indian villages and massacred their inhabitants. Between 1978 and 1985 the regime killed approximately 50,000 to 100,000 civilians. In 1984, Americas Watch, an organization that monitors human rights violations, called Guatemala "a nation of prisoners."

Little has improved in Guatemala despite a return to civilian government with the election of Mario Vinicio Cerezo to the presidency in 1986. His Christian Democratic government has failed to control the army, whose campaigns of terror force hundreds of Guatemalans to flee their homeland each year. Many make their way to the United States.

Like Nicaragua and Guatemala, El Salvador fell under the sway of its military in the 1930s. In 1931, General Maximiliano Martinez staged a coup that placed him in control of the country for almost 50 years. Martinez earned a reputation for ruthlessness and violence. In 1932, for example, Martinez and his army quelled Indian uprisings by massacring as many as 30,000 of the insurrectionists. After *la matanza* (the massacre) many among the surviving Indian population discarded traditional Indian dress and hid their cultural identity to avoid further persecution. For this reason few visible remnants of Indian culture remain in El Salvador today.

During the first decade of Martinez's rule, a U.S. Army officer visiting the capital city of San Salvador noted the disparity between the opulent way of life of the small Salvadoran elite and the seemingly eternal poverty of the masses:

> There appears to be nothing between these high-priced cars and the oxcart with its barefoot attendant. There is practically no middle class.
> . . . Thirty or forty families own nearly everything in the country. They live in almost regal style.
> The rest of the population has practically nothing.

Forty years later, very little had changed. By the early 1970s, the landlessness, unemployment, poverty, and overpopulation that plagued El Salvador had become intolerable. Students, workers, *campesinos* (peasants), and clergy united in opposition to the dictatorship. These coalitions demonstrated in the streets of San Salvador and forcibly occupied public buildings, factories, and large estates in order to call public attention to their cause.

Government violence and repression mounted in response to the increased vehemence of the opposition. In 1977 government troops murdered rural pastor Father Rutilio Grande. The death marked an important turning point in the movement. Outraged by the killing, San Salvador's new archbishop, Oscar Romero,

Salvadorans gather at the tomb of Oscar Romero to honor the former archbishop of El Salvador on the second anniversary of his assassination. Romero's slaying exposed to world view the brutality of El Salvador's regime and sent thousands of Salvadorans fleeing in panic to the United States.

denounced the military regime in unguarded language that no churchman had dared use before, thus bringing the Catholic church into the thick of the struggle. Both protest and repression escalated until October 1979, when junior officers overthrew the government of General Carlos Humberto Romero and installed a ruling council called a junta, which was run jointly by members of the military and civilians.

Many hoped that the coup would mark the end of violence and political oppression in El Salvador, but the civilians in the junta soon resigned. This left control once more to the military, which organized the most sweeping wave of repression against a popular resistance movement since the matanza of 1932. The leaders of the opposition subsequently joined forces and called for armed insurrection, and by January 1980, El Salvador had descended into chaos.

Human rights groups and church organizations claim that since 1980 more than 60,000 people have been assassinated by government security forces. Between 1980 and 1981 more than 21,000 people died at the hands of the death squads—extralegal bands of soldiers, sponsored by government security agencies, who were assigned to murder government opponents on the basis of real or suspected revolutionary associations. The victims have included labor leaders, teachers, students, professionals, political organizers, Catholic priests, nuns, and lay workers. On March 24, 1980, assassins shot Archbishop Romero, a champion of the nation's poor and an outspoken critic of El Salvador's government. After Romero's death thousands of Salvadorans fled the country.

Even a return to constitutional rule and the 1984 election of José Napoleón Duarte as president failed to better the situation. A member of the Christian Democratic party and leader of the junta from 1980 to 1982, Duarte failed to fulfill his campaign promise to bring the death squads to justice. By 1988, El Salvador's economy had deteriorated further and the war had escalated. Duarte and his Christian Democratic party met defeat in local and legislative elections, which brought to power the Nationalist Rebublican Alliance

(ARENA), an organization lying on the extreme right of the political spectrum. In fact, ARENA's founder, Roberto d'Aubuisson, has been implicated in the murder of Archbishop Romero. In 1989, ARENA's presidential candidate Alfredo Cristiani was elected president of El Salvador. Shadowy assassins have continued to terrorize Salvadoran society into the late 1980s. Despite these well-documented abuses, the U.S. government has continued to provide more than $2 million a day in economic and military aid to El Salvador.

At the end of the 1980s, there appeared to be no end in sight to the war, bloodshed, and poverty that define life for so many of Central America's inhabitants. Not surprisingly, entire families daily quit their homeland and the unrelenting hardship of existence there for the hope of a better life elsewhere. The United States was their most common destination, but despite the obstacles that they had to overcome to reach there, they seldom received a warm welcome upon arrival.

On November 25, 1986, Salvadoran president José Napoleón Duarte addressed the General Assembly of the United Nations to plead for economic aid to El Salvador, which had been struck by an earthquake just one month before.

FRANCISCO
Jose Antonio
Lamus
Desaparecido
15 Abril 1983
Por el F.
Nuevo Edén
Comité de
Nuestros Hijos?
Madres

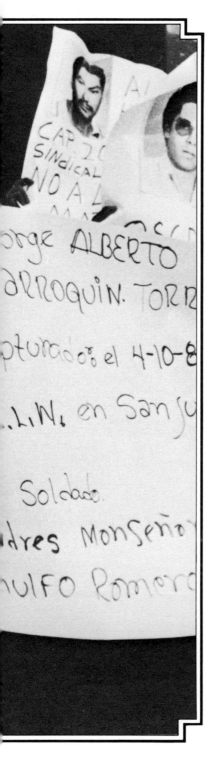

On March 16, 1984, a legion of mothers marches on San Salvador, demanding to know what has become of their missing children and other relatives who were abducted by security squads. The signs they hold bear the names of the missing, along with the date they were kidnapped.

EVENTS OF IMMIGRATION

Since 1980 increasing numbers of Central Americans have been fleeing their countries in search of safety and freedom from persecution. The great majority of these emigrants come from El Salvador and Guatemala, where they have fled the civil strife that has torn those countries for the past decades. Many have suffered from extreme poverty, had their homes destroyed, been forced to serve in the armed forces, and lived with the constant fear that they will be killed. Nearly all have lost a friend or relative to the violence.

In El Salvador and Guatemala, tens of thousands of civilians have been abducted, tortured, or killed by death squads, which international human rights organizations such as Americas Watch and Amnesty International have blamed for much of the violence in those nations. In El Salvador, the government has always maintained that the death squads act independently of the military, but widespread documentation proves that several of the principal death squads work directly for the Salvadoran government's three security forces. Amnesty International has estimated that government-backed assassins killed 40,000 people in El Salvador between 1979 and 1984. Twelve thousand were murdered in 1981 alone. The agency found that the military authorities had sanctioned the vast majority of the killings.

The Dead and the Disappeared

The story of Francisco Nuñez echoes that of many other Salvadorans who have been victims of the death squads. Nuñez helped care for elderly and ill inhabitants in the refugee camps that have sprung up in El Salvador to take care of the large number of people displaced by violence. Such activity brought him to the attention of the government, which deemed him suspect. In 1984, security forces kidnapped Nuñez, his wife, and their two children in the middle of the night and subjected Nuñez to intense physical torture. They also raped his wife and threatened to harm his children. He later told the *Sacramento Bee*: "If they would have accused me of being the one who tried to kill the pope I would have confessed after that."

Five days after Nuñez was first arrested, his captors released him into the custody of the civil police, having obtained his signed confession that he had participated in subversive activities. A judge convicted Nuñez and sentenced him to life imprisonment in Mariona, a Salvadoran jail that houses political prisoners. At that point, the only thing that kept the Nuñez family from abject despair was their knowledge that most of El Salvador's judges would accept bribes in exchange for reversing convictions.

The Nuñezes sold their house and all their possessions, raising the equivalent of $5,000 toward Francisco's release. The judge did agree to free Francisco but, according to the *Bee*, told him, "You'd better leave the country. I won't be responsible for what happens to you after 30 days," meaning that Nuñez would likely be targeted for assassination. He left El Salvador for the United States 10 days later.

Like Francisco Nuñez, most victims of abduction are suspected by the police or the army of being critical of the regime. In order to ferret out "subversives," authorities rely on *orejas* (ears), who inform on the activities of neighbors, colleagues, and even family members. An unfavorable report by an *oreja* often leads directly to illegal arrest. In 1984, *New York* magazine published the story of Luis Dominguez, an agricultural engineer from El Salvador who lived with his wife and three children in a middle-class neighborhood on the outskirts of San Salvador. Soon after Dominguez made critical comments about the corrupt administration of a land-reform program on which he worked, he received a note from the "Anti-Communist Army" warning him to leave the country within two weeks or his body, and the bodies of his wife and children, would be "given to the earth." Several of his colleagues and their families had been executed a few months earlier. Soon after, Dominguez and his family were able to obtain U.S. visas and fly to New York, leaving everything behind.

The stories of Luis Dominguez and Francisco Nuñez closely resemble those of other Salvadorans who survived the terror of the mid-1980s. One woman now living in Los Angeles told researchers that in the middle of the night she would hear gunshots and cries for help as people were killed, raped, or kidnapped by security forces. Salvadorans risked abduction merely by walking down the street, and many—even schoolchildren—left home in the morning and were never seen again. In many cases it was impossible to obtain any information about those who were taken this way. It was as if the victims had simply vanished. In El Salvador and other Central and South American countries the citizenry invented a name for those victims of governmental terror who went unaccounted for. They called them the *desaparecidos*, the "disappeared."

Accounts of death squad activity in Guatemala are equally disturbing. Kanjobal Indians from San Miguel Acatlan, a highland village in western Guatemala near the Mexican border, told researchers in Los Angeles that they had seen fellow villagers dragged off to be murdered or tortured. One said that government soldiers had killed 400 people in his village, including his younger brother, a union organizer. Another said, "I didn't come here [to the United States] for amusement.

At a community health clinic in Usulután, El Salvador, a woman and child survey the damage done to their town. Despite its white flag, a symbol of neutrality, the building in which they stand suffered damage from gunfire.

I came here because there was blood running in the streets of my town."

The number of political killings and death squad activities in Guatemala declined somewhat at the end of the 1980s. After 1986 the police called a halt to the mass slaying of ordinary citizens, in reaction to outcries from the international human rights community. Instead, they targeted activist leaders for execution, killing only a handful every few months. Even the method of disposing of victims' remains changed, reflecting the government's newfound discretion. Whereas the police once abandoned bodies in ditches and side streets, by the end of the decade they had taken to dropping the corpses into lakes or the sea.

The wholesale massacre of Central Americans has stopped for the present, but the memories of mass killings remain fresh in the minds of the populace. Each time a prominent political or religious figure disappears or is discovered dead, a wave of fear passes through Central American society. In this ambience of violence and fear, thousands of Salvadorans and Guatemalans believe they have no choice but to flee their homes and families, seeking safe haven in neighboring countries and the United States.

The Armed Forces

Although the terror engendered by the death squads is the most dramatic of the abuses suffered by Salvadorans and Guatemalans, it ranks as only one among many violations of their human rights perpetrated by their government. Many people lose their friends and

In Judicalpa, Honduras, a United States Army task force trains Honduran soldiers to use a howitzer, a small cannon capable of firing missiles at extremely high speeds. Operation Dragon/ Golden Pheasant was sent to Honduras by President Ronald Reagan to guard against possible invasion by Nicaragua and to train counterrevolutionaries, known as contras, *to fight the Sandinista army.*

family not to death but to forced induction into the army. A veteran observer of Central America told the *National Catholic Reporter* that many young men are simply picked up on street corners and initiated into the army by being made to rape and torture civilians. "But once you start down that road, you can't turn back, because you [are taught to believe that everyone outside the armed forces] is your enemy. . . . I heard them myself in Honduras, recruits marching around the barrack yard and chanting, 'The civilian is my enemy.' "

In Central America only the poor enter the military as enlisted recruits—for many, it is the only job they can find. In El Salvador, peasants and poor urban workers fill the ranks of the army. Many of them act as soldiers with great reluctance and suffer from low morale. An army colonel explained the army's recruitment methods by saying, "In my district, people leave home and become soldiers so they can eat. To fill out the ranks, we go to a football stadium and round them up by force."

Once in uniform, soldiers often follow orders to attack not just individuals but entire peasant villages thought to support El Salvador's leading guerrilla group, the Farabundo Martí Front for National Liberation (or FMLN, named in honor of 1930s Salvadoran revolutionary Augustín Farabundo Martí).

In order to weaken the guerrilla strongholds in the countryside, soldiers have entered villages to burn the peasants' corn and bean crops, destroy hospitals, and kill the peasants themselves. According to the *Dallas Morning News*, in one Salvadoran village under attack a group

> struggled up their steep embankment to the village of Tenange, a few miles south of Pepeishtenango. A37 and Ouragen attack jets hammered them for hours, a spectacle we witnessed from the vantage of our hilltop. The bombardment from strafing killed or wounded roughly 100 elderly, women, and children, dazed survivors later said.

A peasant woman sits inside a church in San Mateo, Guatemala. The country's bankrupt economy has driven more than 250,000 Guatemalans from the countryside and into the slums of Guatemala City or the refugee camps of Honduras and Mexico.

Lives of Poverty

Guatemalans and Salvadorans who survive attacks on their village often find themselves without either crops, a home, or a source of income. In 1984 the Urban Institute estimated that 250,000 to 500,000 Guatemalans were homeless in their own nation, and their counterparts in El Salvador numbered approximately 450,000 to 600,000. In 1986 the number of homeless Salvadorans increased when an earthquake shattered the capital city of San Salvador. Many of those without

Peasant women in San Mateo, Guatemala, haul water up a rocky mountainside in their village. Many villages in Central America lack amenities, such as running water, that most North Americans take for granted, but because the region suffers from continual civil unrest it can not achieve the economic stability that would improve the lives of villagers such as these.

homes have fled to other parts of Central America, to Mexico, and to the United States. A 1985 Urban Institute study estimated that 500,000 to 850,000 Salvadorans have come to the United States, as have 100,000 to 200,000 Guatemalans. Most are undocumented, which means they either entered the United States without an immigration visa or entered with a visa that has expired and have stayed on.

Salvadorans have lost their villages to war and also to rich landowners, who have taken over hundreds of acres of land in rural areas. The growers replant the peasants' fields with cash crops, thus uprooting tens of thousands of subsistence farmers who had been growing basic grains such as corn. In El Salvador the number of landless peasants grew from 12 percent of the rural population in 1961 to 65 percent in 1980.

Many of these displaced campesinos have joined the growing numbers of low-paid agricultural workers who harvest seasonal crops for the rich landowners. Others have been forced to move to the cities, where they seek work in manufacturing, commercial, or construction enterprises or in service occupations such as hotels and restaurants. Although they have fared somewhat better than the friends and neighbors they left behind in the countryside, they must still support themselves on extremely small incomes.

Displaced peasants have flooded the job market with workers for whom no steady employment exists. In Guatemala more than two-thirds of the population cannot find work. Although the number of landless peasants grows each year, landholders refuse to part with the arable land that they do not cultivate, allowing 25 percent of it to lie idle.

Guatemala's high unemployment has been accompanied by soaring inflation. Since the early 1980s these twin blights have driven the Guatemalan economy to the brink of collapse. By 1984 the government was spending twice as much capital as it took in, reaching near bankruptcy by 1985. The country's poor have been forced to bear the worst consequences of Guatemala's economic depression. Lacking land to subsist on, tens of thousands of families have flooded into Guatemala City, where they live in muddy shantytowns.

For many of these homeless people the exodus from the countryside has ended not in urban centers such as Guatemala City and San Salvador, but in the refugee camps of Honduras and Mexico. Still, many human rights and religious organizations believe that violence, not dire poverty, is what ultimately forces peasants out of their country. Researchers who have gained an understanding of refugees report that a majority of Salvadorans and Guatemalans have fled their native land because violence and persecution have forced them to do so.

A family of Salvadoran refugees takes shelter for the night in St. Leo's Catholic Church in Tacoma, Washington. Like hundreds of churches across the United States, St. Leo's belongs to the sanctuary movement and offers aid to undocumented Central American aliens.

SEEKING
SAFE HAVEN

Planning a trip in El Salvador is different from planning one in the United States. Most Salvadorans leaving their country never visit a travel agent, never arrange for a hotel room or a seat on an airplane, and never obtain a passport or visa. Instead, they pack a small bag, quickly bid their friends and family good-bye, and brace themselves for a long journey, usually made on foot and by bus.

The trip from El Salvador, Guatemala, or Nicaragua often begins in a refugee camp or in the border towns of neighboring nations, such as Honduras and Mexico. Since 1980 the number of Central American refugees and displaced persons has grown rapidly as a result of the warfare and unrest in those countries. An Urban Institute study estimates that in 1985, 700,000 to 1.2 million homeless Central Americans lived in their own countries, and an additional 147,000 to 352,000 relocated to refugee camps in other parts of Central America or in Mexico.

Central Americans enter refugee camps either because they have been forcibly evicted from their village by the military or because they have fled their homes to save their lives. In El Salvador, for example, the vast majority of refugees living in camps are women, children, and elderly peasants from rural areas who are trying to find safety from the bombing and fighting near their villages.

Life in the camps is grim. Many provide only the most primitive hovels as shelter and lack running water, proper sanitation, and an adequate supply of fresh food. A 1985 *Sacramento Bee* article described conditions in one of the camps:

> Smoke from cooking fires obscures people huddled across the compound, but their moans can be heard outside the walls. It's the children and the very old who lie in pools of sweat in hammocks, whimpering. The air is hot and heavy with moisture and the pungent smell of illness. . . . In one corner of the camp, a child plays in sewage water.

Most refugee camps receive funds from charitable organizations such as the International Red Cross, church relief programs, and private volunteer groups. The money—which is funneled through the host countries—provides food, shelter, and medical care for people suffering from the many health problems common to refugee camps: malnutrition, skin diseases, diarrhea, parasites, and eye infections. But even funds from abroad cannot alleviate the misery of the camps. In 1984, Mesa Grande, the largest of the camps in Honduras, employed only a staff of 5—2 doctors and 3 nurses—to care for 10,000 people.

Even within the confines of a refugee camp, Central Americans have no guarantee of safety. In El Salvador, Catholic nuns attempt to prevent soldiers from entering a camp and arresting some of its inhabitants. Volunteers at refugee camps work at great risk to their own safety because they often oppose the policies of Central American governments.

Because Honduras borders both El Salvador and Guatemala, refugees usually travel there first and then make their way north into Mexico, where, according to the United Nations High Commission for Refugees, a total of 170,000 refugees arrived in 1984 alone. The influx included 120,000 Salvadorans, 40,000 Guatemalans, and 10,000 other Central Americans.

Mesa Grande—the largest refugee camp in Honduras—houses more than 10,000 people in shoddy structures roofed with corrugated tin.

A Journey of Many Sacrifices

In general, Guatemalan refugees live in camps and settlements in Chiapas, a region of southeast Mexico bordering Guatemala, whereas Salvadorans tend to congregate in and around Mexico City. In fact, Mexico serves as a way station for almost all Central Americans migrating to the United States. For many, the Mexican borders represent the most dangerous part of the journey to the United States because the border patrol is corrupt and unpredictable. Migrants usually have to bribe Mexican immigration authorities, and young Central American women face the danger of being sexually assaulted before they are allowed to enter or leave the country.

A 1987 *New York Times* article reported on the dangers of traveling from El Salvador to the United States. According to the *Times*, a Salvadoran man spent $4,000 on a travel package to bring his wife and 2 young daughters to Los Angeles. The package included a plane ticket for a direct flight from San Salvador to Tijuana, Mexico, followed by an overland trip across the border—led by a smuggler, also known as a *coyote*—ending in a truck ride to a safe house in Los Angeles. The airplane was filled with Salvadorans, all of whom were paying the same smuggler. In Tijuana, the coyote separated the Salvadoran from his wife and daughters, sending the wife with a companion on a perilous hike through the border mountains. The two daughters, ages seven and four, were supplied with false American birth certificates and driven through the INS Border Patrol checkpoint into the United States. All made it safely to Los Angeles.

Despite the well-publicized dangers of these trips, potential emigrants support a thriving business among tour operators, in part because so few Central Americans can obtain legitimate visas to the United States under current U.S. immigration law.

These tour services are usually fronts for profitable smuggling operations that provide transportation and a safe passage across the border. The route and means of transportation differ depending on the fee for the trip. Some offer travel by airplanes, private vans, buses, or trains. Others promise door-to-door delivery from San Salvador to a variety of U.S. cities. Many sell fake documents that smooth an immigrant's way into America, including letters of credit, bank accounts, passports, employment recommendations, and clean police records. A complete package costs about $700, the equivalent of a year's pay for most Salvadorans.

For Central Americans the journey to the United States is *hecho con muchos sacrificios*, "made with many sacrifices." En route to their destination Central Americans often suffer from exhaustion, hunger, thirst, and the abuses of unscrupulous coyotes. In July 1980, for example, a coyote collected his fees and then abandoned 26 Salvadorans in the Arizona desert. Half of them had died of thirst and heat exposure by the time they were found. On July 2, 1987, an equally horrifying fate befell 18 undocumented migrants who were locked in a boxcar on a freight train traveling east from El Paso, Texas, to Dallas and suffocated. The boxcar victims were Mexican rather than Central American, but their suffering helped publicize the danger that all undocumented migrants passing through the American Southwest must face. One of the 18 who died left behind a notebook full of poems, which was discovered by a reporter. Written in Spanish, one was entitled "El Illegal" and read, in part, as follows:

> I didn't leave you a single cent.
> With pain I left my country.
> Today there is talk of the Rio Bravo
> Which I'll cross aboard an old tree root.
> Landed in Texas-Weslaco, San Antonio,
> Houston and Dallas. That was my song.
> Texas is Texas, very big and far apart
> But it all fits inside my heart.

The most perilous leg of the journey north lies along the 2,000-mile border between the United States and Mexico, where people migrating north pass through one of four popular crossing points. Two are at the California border at Tijuana and Mexicali, one is at the Arizona border at Nogales, and one is at the Texas border at Matamoros, a city in the Rio Grande Valley. The closer one gets to the U.S. border, the more dangerous the journey becomes. At Benjamin Hill, for example, 75 miles south of the border crossing in Nogales, a legendary "double checkpoint" awaits migrants. At the first checkpoint the Mexican border patrol extorts enormous bribes from travelers but allows them to continue. At the second checkpoint the migrants are arrested.

The crossing between Matamoros in Mexico and Brownsville in Texas is one of the most important points of entry for Salvadorans. According to the INS Border Patrol, 90 percent of the Salvadorans and Guatemalans entering through this area are smuggled in by coyotes, who charge from $400 to $500 per person to smuggle Central Americans across the Rio Grande. For several hundred more they will take them beyond the dangerous Border Patrol checkpoints to safer territory 50 to 60 miles inland. For an even higher price they will take them all the way to Houston. For many undocumented Central American migrants, their first contact with Americans may be with INS officials, who daily try to stem what they regard as an "invasion"

In July 1980 two members of the U.S. Border Patrol comfort Yolanda Hernandez (left) and Dora Herrera, victims of an unscrupulous "coyote" who abandoned 26 Salvadorans in the desert of southwestern Arizona after bringing them across the United States–Mexico border. Only half the group survived.

from Central America and often resort to illegal violence to do so. *In the Shadow of Liberty*, a 1988 report issued by the American Friends Service Committee on Central American refugees in the United States, quotes a legal aid worker in Texas as saying that Border Patrol agents and police in Texas border regions often commit violence against refugees and that it

> is so prevalent that it leads you to think that it is considered acceptable because it is a deterrent to illegal entry. Refugees and undocumented workers are deprived of the protection of their lives, property, and persons because they are afraid to call the police when assaulted, knowing they will probably be detained and deported.

To many Central American migrants it may appear that there is little difference between those Americans who abuse them and the rest of the population. However, some people seeking safe haven have benefited from the help of Americans willing to risk prison terms and large fines to bring refugees to safety.

The Sanctuary Movement

The sanctuary movement has been compared with the famed Underground Railroad of the pre–Civil War era, a loosely organized system for helping runaway slaves to safety. Consisting of safe houses and havens owned or administered by individuals opposed to slavery, the Underground Railroad carried hundreds of slaves to freedom in the Northern states or Canada. Many of its "conductors" were ministers or members of their congregation. Similarly, in the 1980s a loose network of almost 300 congregations of all denominations has guided hundreds of Central American refugees across the U.S. border to safety. Sanctuary members work with the understanding that they risk jail terms and fines, but they believe that in breaking the law they are saving the lives of innocent people.

Jim Corbett, a retired rancher and a Quaker, is generally regarded as the founder of the sanctuary movement. In 1980 he heard about the Salvadorans who had died in the desert after being abandoned, and he decided to start helping Central American refugees across the Arizona border. Beginning in 1981, Corbett established routes around Mexican immigration checkpoints and since then has helped hundreds, perhaps thousands, of refugees to safety. In 1982 the movement grew when Reverend John Fife of the Southside Presbyterian Church in Tucson declared his church to be a sanctuary for Central American refugees, and hundreds of churches across the country followed suit. In 1984 the sanctuary movement helped 350 undocumented Central Americans settle in the United States.

The sanctuary movement has won widespread support both in the United States and in foreign countries. During a September 1987 visit to America, Pope John Paul II lauded the "great courage and generosity" of those who have protected undocumented Central American immigrants from deportation by the federal government. The pope's sentiments were not shared by the INS, which grew alarmed at the scope and success of the movement. In January 1985 federal authorities indicted 16 sanctuary leaders on charges of smuggling and of conspiring to smuggle undocumented aliens into the United States. In the end, 2 of the 16 workers were convicted and jailed in Texas. The others were released on probation and forbidden to engage in sanctuary work.

Supporters of the sanctuary movement march in Washington, D.C., in 1986 in protest of both U.S. intervention in Central America and domestic policy regarding Central American refugees.

Political or Economic Refugees?

The sanctuary movement in the United States grew out of a desire to help Central Americans enter the country despite the fact that the U.S. government has closed most legal channels of immigration to them. Salvadorans, Guatemalans, and Nicaraguans have two means of remaining in the United States lawfully: They can be granted asylum or extended voluntary departure status.

The government offers asylum only to those individuals who fear political persecution in their home countries. In the view of the United States most Central Americans have no right to asylum status because they face no mistreatment based on their political or religious beliefs. In fact, in the case of El Salvador the U.S. government denies even the existence of a civil war in the region. According to Joseph Flanders, an INS press agent for the California regional office, Salvadorans are "like every other illegal alien. They come here looking for jobs, not to escape the 'war.' The 'war' proved to be false."

Central Americans stand at a disadvantage in gaining asylum also because the United States has always favored immigrants leaving Communist regimes. Over the years, the U.S. government has proved more willing to believe claims of persecution from individuals fleeing the government of one of its ideological enemies in the Communist bloc than from immigrants alleging mistreatment by a government that the United States has propped up with extensive military and fi-

Four children from El Salvador—all 8 to 10 years old—wait in an INS building in Seattle, Washington, while their mothers undergo questioning by immigration officers. The Salvadorans were detained as part of a nationwide crackdown begun by the U.S. government on the sanctuary movement in 1984.

nancial aid. Those seeking asylum must first qualify as refugees, a status that from 1952 to 1980 was defined by law as "a person fleeing from a Communist-dominated country or area, or from any country within the general area of the Middle East." After the passage of the Refugee Act of 1980, Congress altered the definition of "refugee" to accord with that of the United Nations as anyone unable or unwilling to return to his or her country because of persecution or a well-founded fear of persecution "on account of race, religion, nationality, membership in a particular social, group, or public opinion."

Although the wording of the law changed, its spirit remained much the same. Since 1980 the U.S. government has granted entrance to liberal numbers of political refugees from Communist regimes such as those ruling Poland, Afghanistan, and Vietnam. During 1986, for example, only 3 percent of requests for asylum from Salvadorans were approved, as opposed to 90 percent of requests from Poles and 64 percent of requests from Iranians. As these figures show, the INS discourages Central Americans from requesting asylum, even though the United Nations High Commission for Refugees has recognized Salvadorans as a group as refugees. According to one attorney who represents Central Americans before the INS, "for the State Department to say there is enough evidence [to prove persecution], you'd have to bring a dead body and the perpetrator admitting guilt into a courtroom."

Central American refugees who are denied asylum can try to qualify for extended voluntary departure (EVD) status. Granted at the discretion of the attorney general, EVD status allows citizens from war-torn countries to remain in the United States temporarily and obtain a work permit. Unlike asylum status, EVD is granted to an entire group of people, not just individuals.

Various groups, including the American Civil Liberties Union, have unsuccessfully sought this status for Central Americans. But despite the reluctance of the U.S. government to allow Central Americans into the United States, thousands have successfully crossed the border and established communities throughout the country.

A Guatemalan woman prepares tortillas in her home in Washington, D.C., a city with one of the largest populations of Central Americans.

GETTING ESTABLISHED

Like many other immigrant groups, Central Americans tend to settle near communities of people from their own countries. In general, most head for states and cities with large Hispanic populations. California, home to more Hispanics than any other state, holds about half of all Central American immigrants. The other half are scattered from coast to coast. About 10 to 15 percent of Central Americans live in Texas and Washington, D.C., respectively, and an equal number inhabit New York City and its environs. The rest have put down roots in towns and urban centers across the United States.

Waves of Immigration

Until the 1970s the number of Central American immigrants to the United States was relatively small. The first trickle of immigration from the region began in the 19th century. By 1900 about 2,173 Central Americans had settled in the United States; more than 1,000 came each year until the 1930s and the onset of the Great Depression, which virtually halted Central American immigration. After World War II, however, immigration resumed and increased each year until it reached unprecedented heights. In 1970 a record number of Central Americans—174,000 in all—traveled north, but even that amounted to a fraction of the hundreds of thousands of Central Americans who streamed across the U.S. border in the 1970s and 1980s.

In 1967 a group of Salvadoran students flew to San Diego, California, under the auspices of Operation Amigo, an organization promoting friendship between high school students in Latin American countries and their peers in the United States. Until the late 1970s, members of the middle class were virtually the only Central Americans to immigrate to the United States.

Nora Hamilton, a political scientist studying Central Americans in the United States, has divided postwar Central American immigration into three separate waves. The first took place in the 1950s and 1960s and consisted mostly of Panamanians and Hondurans. Most were young men and women from the middle or upper-middle classes who resettled in the United States in order to study at American universities, join the ranks of the U.S. labor force, and in general benefit from the prosperity America enjoyed during this period.

The second wave of immigration took place as a direct result of the political unrest that destabilized El Salvador and Guatemala in the 1970s. The 1969 Soccer War between El Salvador and Honduras—so called because the conflict was touched off by a disputed goal in a soccer match between the two countries—brought thousands of Salvadorans to the United States. In reality the war had little to do with soccer; it began because nearly 300,000 Salvadorans had streamed into Honduras looking for work. The tensions between the two nations caused by the growing number of Salvadorans in Honduras exploded into a border war, and, as a result, the Salvadorans—mostly people from poor families—were expelled from the country. Rather than return to El Salvador, many made their way to the United States in search of work. Many intended to stay only temporarily, but the increase in political violence in their homeland compelled them to remain permanently in America and to send for their families to join them.

The third wave of Central American immigration began in 1980 with a new influx of Central Americans. Seeking refuge from the violence of their homelands, the new group included Nicaraguans as well as Salvadorans and Guatemalans. Unlike earlier arrivals these refugees were classified as "undocumented aliens" because many entered the country through illegal means. By the late 1980s their numbers were estimated to have reached between 600,000 and more than 1 million, but even that approximation is open to question because so many live in secrecy.

Nicaraguans in Miami, Florida, find temporary shelter in a sports arena. Nicaraguans compose the fourth largest Central American ethnic group in the United States and are well represented in the third wave of immigration from Central America, which began in the 1980s.

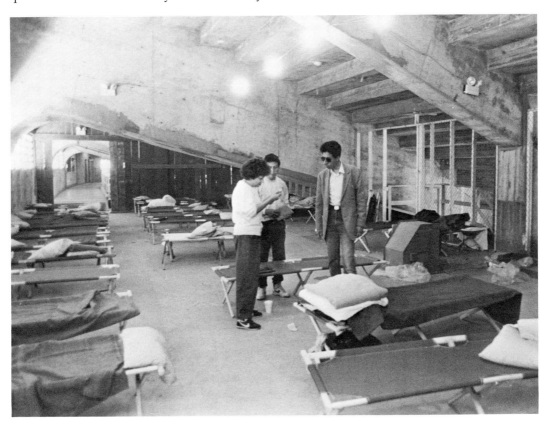

A Question of Numbers

No one knows exactly how many Central Americans now reside in the United States. Most experts rely on three sources in order to estimate the Central American population here: the 1980 U.S. census, reports issued by the Immigration and Naturalization Service, and a study published in 1985 by the Urban Institute. But the numbers cited in these publications vary widely. Although the U.S. census claimed that 319,243 Central Americans lived in the United States, the Urban Institute set the figure at anywhere between 750,000 and 1.3 million. Some of the discrepancy may be attributed to the fact that the census preceded the Urban Institute study by five years and that the latter document included undocumented as well as documented immigrants.

According to the Urban Institute, the Central American community in the United States includes small numbers of immigrants from Costa Rica, Belize, and Panama; 40,000 to 80,000 Nicaraguans; 50,000 to 100,000 Hondurans; 100,000 to 200,000 Guatemalans, and 500,000 to 850,000 Salvadorans, a great many of whom have settled in Los Angeles.

Los Angeles

After San Salvador, Los Angeles is the second largest Salvadoran city in the world. Most estimates place the number of Salvadorans in the area at 250,000 to 350,000. Also living there are 80,000 to 110,000 Guatemalans, or about half of those in the United States, and an estimated 15,000 Hondurans.

Most Central Americans in Los Angeles inhabit the Pico-Union section, a neighborhood of five square miles located just west of the city's downtown area. In many ways this district is as depressing as the refugee camps with which many of the immigrants are already familiar. Much of the housing is dilapidated, filthy, and infested with rats and other vermin. The neighborhood suffers too from an epidemic of drug abuse and crime. This environment, although alien to Salvadorans and Nicaraguans, is perhaps worst for Gua-

(continued on page 73)

NEW LIVES
IN A NEW LAND

Overleaf: A young Salvadoran mother and her American-born son at The Peruvian Room, a Hispanic restaurant in the Northwest section of Washington, D.C. The mother lives in a crowded apartment with her family while she attends school and dreams of a better life for herself and her son.

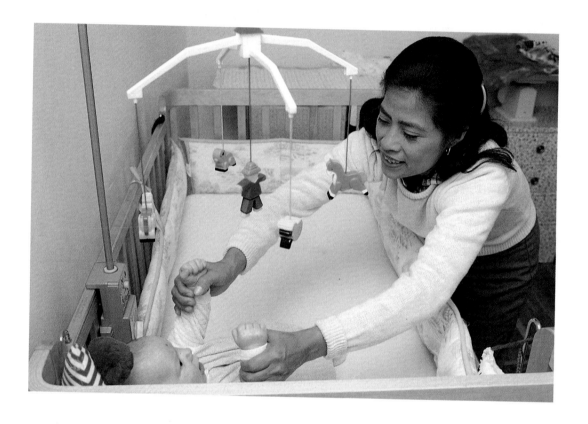

Immigration and resettlement in the
United States often take their toll
on family life, traditionally the center
of Central American society. Many
women, such as this immigrant from
Nicaragua (left) who lives in
Washington, D.C., must work as
domestic servants or nannies and leave
their own children in the care of
neighbors or friends. However, most
young Central American children, such
as these Salvadoran boys and girls in
Los Angeles (at right, top and bottom),
have readily adjusted to the customs
and way of life of the United States.

Central Americans have worked hard to establish a variety of self-help groups
that provide services such as temporary housing, job information, and food and
clothing for new arrivals and also impart a sense of unity to Central American
communities across the country. In Los Angeles, a volunteer from CARE-CEN
(Central American Refugee Center), the largest group devoted to aiding
Central Americans, teaches an English class (above), while a new immigrant
receives help from the Refugee Assistance Program (top left). In Washington,
D.C., a group of Central American domestic workers meet to discuss
employment opportunities (bottom left).

Central Americans have opened many small businesses. Guatemala House (upper right) in Washington, D.C., owned by Carlos Rojas, sells Central American clothing, jewelry, and decorations and also includes an income tax preparation business. The Elizabeth Beauty Salon (bottom right), in the Adams-Morgan section of Washington, D.C., is owned and operated by Elizabeth Rosales from El Salvador. Her husband, Mauricio, is a goldsmith and runs a jewelry counter at the back of the salon. Although the majority of Central Americans are employed as unskilled laborers, some manage to obtain more lucrative positions, such as this man from Belize (below) who is a new-accounts representative at a Los Angeles bank.

Central American laborers pick lettuce in Orange County, California. Working conditions are difficult and employment opportunities scarce for undocumented Central Americans, yet they have endured the hardships and established new lives for themselves. Many hope to further their education and get better jobs, thereby ensuring a brighter future for themselves and their families.

(continued from page 64)

temalans, who are adjusting not only to another country but to another century.

A large portion of the Guatemalans in Los Angeles are descendants of the Maya. Many have lost their land or are avoiding conscription into the Guatemalan army. A smaller percentage of the immigrant population in Los Angeles—1,500 to 3,000 individuals in all—consists of Kanjobal Indians from the Guatemalan highlands. Because most modern technology was unknown to the Kanjobal, they have suffered from culture shock to a greater degree perhaps than any other Central American immigrant group. Many had never used electricity or traveled in a bus or car before leaving home. Terrified by the fast pace and potential dangers of life in Los Angeles, many Kanjobal women responded by locking themselves and their children inside their apartments.

The Kanjobals' isolation was intensified because most did not speak English or Spanish but two Indian dialects. The inability to communicate prevented them from performing such basic tasks as reading street signs, buying food and other necessities, and communicating with potential employers or doctors. These disadvantages have helped unify the Kanjobal com-

This bakery employs Guatemalan immigrants in Los Angeles's Pico-Union neighborhood, home to approximately half a million Central Americans.

munity. Families from the same region try to live close to one another in Los Angeles so that they can come to each other's assistance on a daily basis. The same is true in the migrant camps of California, where Kanjobals often labor as agricultural workers during the harvest season.

The Nicaraguans

If the Kanjobals occupy one end of the spectrum of Central American refugees, Nicaraguans reside at the other. In contrast to the Kanjobal, rural Guatemalans of modest means, recent Nicaraguan immigrants tend to be members of what was once the country's urban

Nicaraguan refugees check into a shelter at the Bobby Madura Stadium in Miami, Florida. The Nicaraguan community in Miami includes people on both ends of the political spectrum— those who supported the Somoza regime and those who welcomed the Sandinista revolution.

middle class. According to a February 27, 1989, article in the *New York Times* about a detention center in Texas:

> The Nicaraguans encountered at the detention center reflect the depth of their country's crisis. They include an electrical engineer, a shoe factory owner, a lawyer and a university professor. They are unlike the majority of Latin American immigrants and instead resemble the middle- and upper-class Cubans who fled to Miami soon after [Cuba's Communist leader] Fidel Castro took power in 1959.

Like the Cubans, many Nicaraguans make their home in Miami, Florida, where they constitute the largest segment of Florida's Central American community. As of June 1985 between 30,000 and 40,000 Nicaraguans—about half the total population in the United States—resided in Florida's Dade County, which includes Miami. Two distinct waves of Nicaraguan immigrants came to Miami between 1979 and 1989. The first immediately preceded the overthrow of the Somoza regime in July 1979, when as many as 20,000 members of Nicaragua's ruling class fled the country for the United States. Most of these immigrants—who ranged in age from approximately 30 to 50—settled comfortably in Miami and had no problem finding employment because they were educated and possessed professional skills. They also benefited from a ready welcome by the United States government, which granted asylum and work permits to approximately 80 percent of the Nicaraguans who requested them.

Throughout the 1980s, Miami's Nicaraguan community changed as new arrivals made their way to Florida. These later immigrants bore little resemblance to the Somoza supporters of 1979, except that they also came in reaction to the Sandinista revolution and to the contra war that followed it. Nearly 80 percent of the Nicaraguan refugees who came to Miami in the early 1980s were young single men—some just 14 years old—fleeing military service in the Sandinista armed forces. This new type of refugee received a cooler reception from the U.S. government, which rejected about 90 percent of their requests for asylum.

The government altered its policy toward Nicaraguan refugees a number of times during the 1980s, first liberalizing regulations, then tightening them. In July 1987, for example, Attorney General Edwin Meese ruled that Nicaraguans must not be deported and that those seeking work permits were entitled to them. According to the *New York Times*, Meese ordered the INS to "encourage and expedite Nicaraguan applications for work authorizations." Some 18 months later, President Ronald Reagan overruled Meese's directive by saying that Nicaraguans were not uniformly welcome in the United States just because they sought to escape what he termed "a Communist regime."

The American change in attitude toward Nicaraguan refugees has dismayed those who have come in the most recent wave of immigration—middle-class opponents of the Sandinista regime and those fleeing the violence of the contra war. Many of these people have friends and relatives in Miami but are having trouble making it that far east. As of February 1989 a government policy required that all Central Americans remain at the Texas border—in towns such as Brownsville, Texas—until granted asylum. Many Central Americans, including a growing number of Nicaraguans, claim that the United States has no right to keep them crowded into towns ill equipped to hold thousands of extra people. Still, Nicaraguans endure the discomfort in the hope of gaining asylum and continuing on to Miami. Amanda Gutiérrez, a Nicaraguan seeking asylum, told *New York Times* reporter Robert Suro: "I cannot believe that this nation . . . will turn us away. But now I have nowhere else to go. I will stay here legally or illegally as long as the Sandinistas are in power."

A Quest for Shelter

Upon arrival in the United States, most Central Americans—whether they are Nicaraguans in Miami or Salvadorans in Los Angeles—rely on a network of friends and relatives who offer them a bed and hot meals,

In Washington, D.C., a homeless Salvadoran man sleeps in the basement of an apartment building because no shelter can accommodate him for the evening. Many Central Americans have trouble finding housing when they first arrive in the United States and stay with friends or relatives until they have saved enough money to rent their own apartment.

assist them in finding jobs, and orient the new arrivals to public transportation and other unfamiliar aspects of life in their new country. Immigrant households often include friends as well as relatives, and as many as 17 to 20 people may live in a single-room apartment. One researcher found that in some cases people run immigrant rooming houses out of their apartments. Women generally operate these businesses, renting beds for eight-hour periods (to coincide with work shifts) and cooking meals for their boarders.

Immigrants who manage to rent their own apartments frequently are victimized by landlords who exploit their fear of detection by immigration authorities. A landlord can intimidate a tenant into paying more rent or living without water by threatening to report him to INS officials. The tyranny of landlords is reflected in the rents charged in the Pico-Union district, where the monthly rate for an apartment can exceed that obtained in prime Los Angeles neighborhoods. With few alternatives available to them, Central Americans endure such difficulties in the hope that by finding a job and working hard they will someday be able to put such exploitation behind them.

The Working World

Before undertaking their journey to America, many Salvadorans and Guatemalans expect to find work in the "land of plenty" almost immediately. In reality, they quickly learn that jobs—particularly full-time positions—are hard to come by, especially for campesi-

Central American men congregate on a street corner in the Pico-Union district of Los Angeles and wait for potential employers needing unskilled laborers to drive by. These work assignments often pay below minimum wage and offer no job security, but Central American immigrants snatch them up because they have few options.

nos unfamiliar with city life. Many learn about employment opportunities from friends or through churches and community centers. In Los Angeles new immigrants often find work at one of the stores or businesses owned by Central Americans in Pico-Union and other neighborhoods. These enterprises include grocery stores, income tax preparation services, religious articles and herb stores (called *botanicas*), dance halls, and bookstores. Some Central Americans operate produce stands out of trucks, from which they sell fresh fruits and vegetables at freeway entrances and exits.

Most Central Americans wind up in unskilled part-time or temporary nonunion jobs as gardeners, domestics, factory hands, janitors, construction workers, and hotel and restaurant employees. Groups of men without regular employment often find day jobs by rising early and standing on a designated street corner, waiting for someone needing laborers to drive up. If work in Los Angeles proves impossible to find, some Central Americans—especially Guatemalans—migrate to California's San Joaquin Valley or to Florida, where they labor as seasonal farm workers.

Central American women often find work more easily than do men, mostly as domestic servants in affluent neighborhoods, where they receive $75 to $120 for a week's work—barely enough to live on. The wages are little better in the Los Angeles garment industry, located near the Pico-Union area. Here women sew on industrial machines in small factories and supplement their income by taking home piecework, so called because it pays on a piece-by-piece rather than an hourly basis. As with men, women prefer being paid in cash so that their undocumented status will remain undetected.

Many Central Americans are forced to labor under conditions outlawed long ago. Unwilling to risk involvement with any sort of governmental or police authority because of their status as illegal aliens, they are often taken advantage of by unscrupulous employers. Under the threat of dismissal, many are paid less than the legal minimum wage and are made to work long hours without rest or meal breaks in unventilated and poorly lit sweatshops. For example, one Central American woman who cleaned buildings from 6:00 P.M. to 8:00 A.M. was forbidden to eat during her shift and became sick as a result of inadequate nutrition. Most workers resent such exploitation, but attempts to form unions or join together in collective action usually end with a factory or store owner calling the INS and revealing the identity of the troublesome immigrants. Without unions, the workers stand little chance of improving their conditions or wages, which fall far below acceptable limits. A 1985 Urban Institute study found that the average household income for Salvadorans in Los Angeles was $370 per month, or less than $4,500 per year—only about half the amount defined as poverty level in the United States.

Even those men and women with an education and professional experience complain of employment difficulties. Because they are undocumented, university professors, accountants, attorneys, doctors, and architects must resign themselves to working as dishwashers, waiters, janitors, and maids. One Salvadoran schoolteacher who now works as a janitor explains, "Our need to survive forces us to accept this kind of work. It is hard and barely covers our living expenses, but we can't afford to look for better jobs." Most employers who discover that a worker possesses professional skills simply try to benefit from this ability

A Salvadoran woman carries dishes through a storage room at a Washington, D.C., restaurant specializing in Salvadoran and Mexican food. Many Central American immigrants support themselves by working in hotel kitchens and restaurants because the jobs require no English and are easy to come by.

without paying more. For example, an accountant working as a seamstress might be given bookkeeping duties but still be paid only seamstress's wages.

After the passage of the Immigration Control and Reform Act of 1986, low-paying, unskilled jobs became even harder to find for undocumented workers. The new law penalizes employers who knowingly hire illegal aliens. Large and small employers, whether factories with hundreds of hands or households employing a single servant, are required to document the legality of all employees. Employers convicted of violating the statute face prison terms and fines of up to $10,000. Many observers believe that the greatest effect of the new law will be to drive undocumented workers further underground and make them more vulnerable to exploitation. Given the incredible determination and perseverance that Central Americans have demonstrated in making their way to the United States and forging a new life, it seems unlikely that the legislation will either convince those immigrants already here to return home or deter future immigration.

After the passage of the Immigration Control and Reform Act of 1986, many immigrants lost even illegally held jobs and earned a living by starting their own small businesses. Here, women prepare a Salvadoran version of fast food to sell at a soccer game in Washington, D.C.

Children at El Rescate (The Refuge), a Central American community organization, get acquainted with the basic tools of American elementary school: Crayola crayons and Elmer's glue.

FACING THE CHALLENGES

Salvadorans and Guatemalans in the United States have found that their experience as immigrants bears little resemblance to that of other groups because so many live in America without official sanction. Every aspect of their lives in the United States is affected by their lack of documentation. This shadowy status makes the life of Central Americans more difficult in two ways: It burdens them with constant worry and disqualifies them from the many government programs that benefit other immigrant groups—such as the Vietnamese—who have been granted refugee status. Aid to refugees typically includes free English classes, employment counseling and job training, and day care—all of which can prove crucial for immigrants adjusting to a new culture.

A Salvadoran woman who was anonymously interviewed for "Voices in Exile," a National Public Radio series about Central American refugees, had this to say: "The government doesn't help at all here. To them, we are worth nothing. They look at us as if we were garbage. As they say here, we are in the belly of the beast. What protection could we have from this government? None at all."

American society itself sometimes seems as incomprehensible as the policies of the U.S. government.

Many Central Americans find the differences between their expectations and the reality of life in America quite striking. "I thought [in Los Angeles] I would be living with Americans, lots of blonds speaking English and playing baseball, but it looked just like Mexico to me," said another Salvadoran heard on "Voices in Exile." Yet another refugee interviewed for the same series commented: "I had expected the United States to be what everybody in El Salvador says it is. They say, 'It's the most beautiful place. There are refrigerators, modern buses that run on electricity and need no gas. Everyone dresses beautifully and has piles of clothes, and money is found in the streets.' [After] time passed and I got used to the situation here in this country, I began to see how this country really is for us."

Separation from their homeland and people leaves many Salvadorans homesick and disoriented. A Salvadoran woman, also interviewed on "Voices in Exile," said, "In the big city, everything seems strange. I was afraid to go out. I didn't *want* to go out. I didn't talk to anybody. I felt very bad." Central Americans often suffer too from the psychological effects of witnessing violence or experiencing it firsthand. Traditionally, they have sought comfort from these traumas by retreating into the safety of their family, but even that succor has been denied them by the violence, which has left few families intact. Once in the United States, Central Americans feel the loss of their families even more profoundly.

La Familia

In Central America, as in all Hispanic cultures, the family—known in Spanish as *la familia*—often includes not only parents and children but also grandparents, aunts and uncles, and cousins, all of whom provide economic and emotional support for each other. Although some families have remained undivided throughout the ordeals of immigration and resettlement, the majority have been torn apart. The violence in El Salvador and Guatemala has severed ties between spouses, children, siblings, and parents. A typical Central American household in the United States might include one parent and one or more children,

Women form the backbone of the Central American family. Many work long hours as domestic servants in other people's homes, thus providing their own household with its steadiest source of income. These jobs leave Central American women with little free time, yet they are still expected to care for their own children, often with minimal help from their husbands.

an aunt or uncle, cousins, and perhaps friends from the homeland.

One young man admitted, "The unity of the family was destroyed. I came to San Francisco, one of my brothers is in L.A., another is in Guatemala, others are in different towns in El Salvador. So we are not together anymore. That destroyed our family. Not only our family, but thousands of families."

In America, family cohesion is further strained by the difference in tasks traditionally performed by men and women. In Central America many mothers stay at home, caring for children and a household. In the United States, many Central American women work as domestic servants and thus do not have the same time to devote to their sons, daughters, and husband. Salvadoran and Guatemalan women are often forced to leave their small children with family members or a neighbor or to pay for child care. If they are live-in maids, they leave their children with a family member and may be able to see them only one day out of the week. Often, even women who live at home have little time to spend with their children because of the long commute they must make to their job each day.

Central American women must also struggle with the demands of their husbands as well as those of their children and employers. Many are physically abused by husbands who have grown angry and frustrated with the constant struggle for employment. Incidents of battering increase when men fall victim to the alcohol and drug abuse so common in poor neighborhoods. In cities such as Los Angeles, hot lines for battered women receive a great number of calls each year from Central Americans.

The Younger Generation

Among Central American immigrant families, the conflict between husband and wife is often mirrored in stormy relationships between parents and children. Central American mothers and fathers often discover that their children are quick to adjust to life in America and demand the greater freedom that their American peers enjoy. "It looks like parents don't have much authority over their children," said a Salvadoran mother heard on "Voices in Exile." "Sometimes they are libertines, and that's no good. I don't know how a 15-year-old can put other things before his parents. I don't like that, and this is a question of [the well-being of the entire] family, it seems to me."

Immigrant teenagers, who have been steeped in a Latin culture, often feel alienated from children they meet in school. Attitudes about dating, for example, differ dramatically. Young women in Central and

South America are often cloistered from the opposite sex, and any social activities between males and females are carefully monitored by parents and older relatives. "For our 13-year-old daughter the change has been terrible," said one Salvadoran mother, also interviewed on "Voices in Exile." "When she talks to girls her age, they have an entirely different way of thinking."

When Central American families first arrive in the United States, they rarely rush to enroll their children in school because other concerns—matters of survival such as food and shelter—seem more pressing. Parents must also get used to the idea that their children are required to go to school and cannot spend their days selling newspapers or otherwise earning income for the family, as they might have done back home. Perhaps the greatest reason for the reluctance to send

Central American teenage girls converse outside their high school in Los Angeles. Teenagers from Central America often feel alienated from their American and Mexican-American peers because they have spent most of their life in a different culture.

children to school is the dread of detection by immigration authorities. This fear abated in 1982 when the Supreme Court ruled in *Phyler vs. Doe* that children of undocumented migrants are entitled to a free public education, which means that immigrant parents are not required to show proof of citizenship.

Enrollment in school can cause various dilemmas for Central American students. One problem is that they are placed in grades by age, just as American children are, even though many have received only sporadic schooling. For example, an 11-year-old Salvadoran placed in a sixth-grade class might have attended school until he or she was 7, worked for 2 years, and then spent another 2 years in a refugee

Young Central American immigrants attend a bilingual class in English and Spanish at a junior high school in Washington, D.C. Programs such as these ease the transition from Latin American countries to the United States and help Central American students of all ages adjust to their new surroundings.

camp. Many Central American children have never been to school at all. Older pupils must adjust not only to a change in routine but also to a shift in role. Many students—especially teenagers—resent being treated as children because they functioned as adults in Central America. Teenagers who have been breadwinners for their families or have run with bands of guerrilla troops and been taught to handle automatic weapons are loath to be sentenced to detention for handing in their homework late.

Younger and older pupils alike struggle to learn English, which is usually not taught in Central American public schools. Because it stigmatizes Central American students as newcomers and outsiders, the language barrier can cause social as well as educational problems. Immigrant children may be ridiculed as "wetbacks" or "TJs" (from Tijuana). A Salvadoran schoolgirl told National Public Radio that

> the Mexican girls in school would want to fight with me for nothing. "Let's fight, wetback," they'd say, just to fight. "Let's fight, damn wetback." I think, what is happening? They told me it means that I am illegal. When one is in school, that word is known by the blacks and whites. It's the word they learn first in Spanish—*mojado*—or bad words to offend you. So I felt real bad.

In trying to assimilate, students often mask traits that reveal them as foreign. For example, Jorge Orellana, a Salvadoran student in a Chicago school, says his classmates taunted him as a "Mexican kid." He now introduces himself as George.

A Need to Heal

In general, young Central Americans adjust to life in the United States more quickly than do adults. Still, many have sustained profound psychological damage from years of exposure to violence. In "Characteristics of Central American Migration to Southern California," a joint study by political scientist Nora Hamilton and sociologist Norma Chinchilla, the authors discuss a Salvadoran girl who awoke in the middle of the night to the sound of her father pleading, "Help me!" She heard a burst of gunfire and minutes later her mother came into the room and told her, "Your father has been killed. You are not to cry. We will be leaving in a few hours."

In some cases, children are spirited out of the country by their parents and sent to America to live with relatives they have never met or barely know. As a result of these sudden changes, many children feel great sadness, especially if they have been separated from their parents. According to Dr. William Arroyo, a psychiatrist who has studied the effects of violence on Salvadoran children: "When kids arrive here they're mourning the loss of their country, their food, their customs. And they're much poorer here. Some don't eat for several days or have only what's provided at school, and only during the week. The fear of being deported is chronic and stressful."

According to Arroyo many young people have been traumatized by what they have seen or experienced in El Salvador and suffer from posttraumatic stress disorder syndrome, a psychological condition also experienced by soldiers after they return from war. Some of the children have lost friends and relatives before their eyes and are haunted by nightmares of war, torture, and death. Those separated from their families worry continuously about their parents, siblings, and relatives still at home. Many children and teenagers have been saddled with responsibilities that would overwhelm even adults—getting themselves and a younger sibling to safety, for example—and crumble beneath the strain of this situation once they have reached a safe haven.

Children and teenagers also suffer from guilt at having survived a situation that took the life of friends and family. In an article in the *Los Angeles Times*, Dr. Arroyo told the story of Juan, a 10 year old from El Salvador, who was unable to sleep or concentrate on his schoolwork because he was so depressed. He also experienced recurrent nightmares in which his mother called to him. He told Dr. Arroyo of a night when "the

death squad, seven men masquerading in women's clothes, ransacked our house and threatened to kill all of us. My mother was screaming, 'Kill me, kill me, but please don't kill my children.' " She was shot dead.

According to Dr. Arroyo, it is possible for children to recover "if life for [them] before all this trauma was good, and if life afterward is good, if one gets to address these fears and concerns with some empathetic and willing listener who encourages discussion." He tells of a six year old who was basically unable to function, so fearful that she would not even bathe unless her father or grandmother was in the bathroom. After several months of counseling, she was able to go to school.

Adults also suffer from psychological disorders such as acute depression, anxiety, loneliness, and con-

Dr. William Arroyo visits an El Rescate center to counsel a young Central American refugee. Psychological trauma affects many Central American children but can be alleviated through therapy and the resumption of a normal life.

A drawing by a nine-year-old Guatemalan girl in a Mexican refugee camp illustrates the violence many children have witnessed in Central America. Victims of brutal regimes, no matter what their age, can experience such psychological disturbances as recurring nightmares, anxiety, and paralyzing depression years after they have escaped physical danger.

fusion. Dr. Richard Mollica, codirector of the Harvard Program in Refugee Trauma at the Harvard University School of Public Health, says many torture victims and refugees have problems as complex and profound as those suffered by survivors of Nazi concentration camps. A psychiatrist working with Central American refugees in Los Angeles explains, "People do not realize how hard off these people are. It is not the same as early waves of emigrants who came to the Northeast with families to support them. These people have survived horrendous overland treks and suffered a breakdown of family and community life."

Most people find their separation from family, village, and country the most distressing aspect of their immigration. In the doctoral dissertation "Migration and Acculturation Processes of Undocumented El Salvadorans in the San Francisco Bay Area" by Carlos Cordova, a Salvadoran identified only as "Jorge" says, "It's like a dream. I wake up in the morning and here I am in San Francisco while in reality I want to be in El Salvador. Sometimes I dream of the war and I wake up here, and finally I feel safety, but I am here alone. And I ask myself if it is really worth it." Many refugees are plagued by nightmares about friends and relatives who have died. According to an article published in March 1986 in *Image*, the Sunday magazine of the *San Francisco Examiner*, a young Salvadoran named Salvador Hernandez talks in his dreams to a friend who was killed: "[I see] Felipe, a young boy who 'disappeared,' and when I see him I am afraid, because I know he is dead. But Felipe says to me, 'No, it's just a rumor.' "

Salvadorans and Guatemalans must recover from physical as well as psychological ailments. Children and pregnant women have the most serious health problems because they require the best nutrition. The list of the most common maladies includes tropical diseases such as malaria and parasites, inflammation of the lining of the stomach and intestines, malnutrition, and tuberculosis. Other difficulties frequently involve injuries received during torture and can produce chronic pain or the partial loss of vision or hearing.

Although many Central Americans require the immediate attention of a doctor, few seek professional health care for a number of reasons. They mistrust officials in institutions such as hospitals and clinics because they fear being turned in to the INS. Proper health care simply does not fit into the frame of reference of most Central American immigrants because few in Central America—and especially El Salvador—regard it as a high priority. Those with emotional rather than physical complaints are even more reluctant to seek out help because of the stigma attached to mental illness.

Because so few refugees can afford the high cost of health care, many seek help from community refugee

A Central American man speaks with a doctor at Clinica del Pueblo, a free medical clinic for Central Americans located in Washington, D.C.

centers, which provide free care, and from low-cost clinics. In the Pico-Union district of Los Angeles, the Oscar Romero Clinic is the only health facility that caters specifically to Central Americans. Funded by private donations, the clinic often turns away patients because of a shortage of medical personnel. In San Francisco, the Father Moriarity Central America Refugee Project provides some medical services at its clinic but not enough to adequately service the city's entire Central American community.

In lieu of modern methods of health care, many Central Americans fall back on the folk medicine tradition they practiced at home. In Central America many illnesses are seen as having supernatural or magical origins. Patients receive ritual treatments and take remedies prescribed by the *sobador* or *curandero* (witch doctor) or healers who use teas, *remedios* (remedies), and medicines extracted from herbs and other plants. These ancient healing techniques represent just one of the many traditions of Central America that refugees have brought with them to the United States.

Leisure Time

Because Central Americans find so many differences between their culture and that of Americans, they tend to avoid "outsiders" and look for entertainment and companionship within their own communities. Within those neighborhoods there is a world of social and athletic activity. Adults dance the rumba and salsa to dance hall bands, which also give concerts of popular Latino music. Special events within the community often attract the attention of the mainstream press and the public. Each year Salvadorans in Los Angeles hold a Miss El Salvador beauty contest. In San Francisco's Mission District, the annual 24th Street Cultural Festival showcases the area's diverse Hispanic population. The 1986 festival drew more than 100,000 people.

The social life of Central American immigrants is further enriched by an active media and by athletics. In cities with large Hispanic populations, such as Los Angeles and San Francisco, radio and television stations air Spanish-language programs and movies. These programs enable Central Americans to keep abreast of the news both at home and in their new environment. Sports fans listen to news about community athletics with particular interest and are especially eager to learn the latest scores for soccer—the most popular sport in Central America. Central Americans have organized several soccer leagues in the United States, such as the El Salvador Soccer League in Los Angeles, which has 19 teams. Guatemalans also have their own league.

Many Central Americans are also involved in political organizations that run the gamut from ultracon-

A father plays with his baby daughter during an outing in a Los Angeles park. Central Americans have little time and money for recreation and try to take part in fun but inexpensive activities that the whole family can enjoy.

servative to ultraliberal. They support the policies of the various political factions in their homelands through political speeches, rallies, marches, and demonstrations. As in Central America, political debate often descends into violence. Since July 1987 a reign of terror begun by right-wing Salvadoran supporters of the Salvadoran military has deeply frightened refugees and activists in Los Angeles. Groups modeling themselves after death squads kidnapped two activist Central American women, one of whom was raped and tortured. Many fear that right-wing forces have infiltrated local community groups, targeting fellow Salvadorans for the kind of terror that originally caused many refugees to flee their homeland. Both the

Federal Bureau of Investigation and the Los Angeles Police Department have been called in to investigate the violence.

The influx of former Salvadoran military men into the United States illustrates a point often forgotten by the American public: Not all Central Americans are refugees hostile to the governments of their homelands. For example, right-wing candidates for election in El Salvador campaign for funds in Los Angeles. They avoid the Pico-Union district, holding campaign banquets elsewhere to attract affluent Americans who share their political beliefs. Some middle-class Salvadorans who have been here a long time are unsympathetic to the Salvadoran revolution, believing it is controlled by Communists from Cuba and Nicaragua. Unlike the refugees of the 1980s, they do not dream of someday returning to their homeland.

Central American mothers and their children visit El Hogar de la Familia (The Family Place), a community center in Washington, D.C., where refugees drop in for advice about obtaining an application for asylum, finding medical care, or enrolling their children in the local schools.

TOWARD A
BRIGHTER FUTURE

Most people studying the lives of Salvadorans, Guatemalans, and Nicaraguans
in the United States overlook the accomplishments and contributions of these groups and fo-
cus instead on their struggles. But despite the myriad
hardships they have endured, Central Americans have
managed to build communities in the United States
and have enriched this nation's culture by doing so.
Their efforts to help themselves overcome dire circum-
stances are a model of community activism at its best.

Some Central Americans, particularly Salvadorans,
worked as community organizers in their homeland
and have brought their skills with them to Pico-Union
and other Central American neighborhoods. In the
United States they create self-help groups that assist
refugees by providing them with temporary housing,
job information, food and clothing, English classes,
and referrals to doctors and immigration lawyers.
These groups also host religious festivals and social
gatherings that help communities maintain a sense of
unity.

The Central American Refugee Center (CARE-
CEN)—the largest group devoted to aiding Central
Americans—claims branches in several U.S. cities, in-
cluding Los Angeles, San Francisco, New York, and

Washington, D.C. Other organizations providing similar services include El Rescate in Los Angeles and the Central American Refugee Committee (CRECE) in San Francisco. In addition, groups act as advocates for the community by educating and informing Americans about the refugees. Members of groups such as CRECE give presentations in churches, schools, and other public forums that provide testimony as to why Central Americans fled their homeland and describe their life in the United States. Many community advocates, such as Felipe Excot, a Guatemalan of Mayan descent, believe they need to speak out "to raise the consciousness of the American people to what is happening in Central America."

As Americans learn more about the plight of Central American refugees, many respond with assistance efforts of their own. As Douglas Carranza, a Salvadoran, put it, "The American people who live here may not be informed, but they have big hearts. When you talk to them, they try to help. Republican or Democrat, it doesn't matter. They understand when we explain." Through churches and other community organizations, many Americans are lending a hand,

Refugees gather in the waiting room of a CARE-CEN office. CARE-CEN is the largest group devoted to helping Central Americans in the United States and has branches across the country.

whether by donating medical or legal services, providing housing, clothing, and food, or by other means. Some even travel to El Salvador and Guatemala to help with relief efforts there.

Cultural Impact

The presence of Central Americans in the United States has greatly increased public knowledge of the politics and culture of the region. Film studios and the television industry have reflected a greater awareness of Salvadorans and their neighbors by presenting a large array of works with Central American themes. In the fall of 1987, for example, the American Broadcasting Company (ABC) aired "I Married Dora," a situation comedy about a Salvadoran refugee who marries her employer, a conservative widower with children, in order to remain legally in the United States. More sober views on Central American life have included public television documentaries about the Central American community in the United States and several movies, including *Salvador* and *Under Fire*, a motion picture set in Nicaragua during the downfall of the Somoza regime.

One of the most powerful films to date on the plight of Central American refugees is *El Norte*, released in 1983. American filmmakers Gregory Nava and Anna Thomas drew on actual experiences of Kanjobal Indians living in Los Angeles to present the story of two young Guatemalan Indians, a brother and sister, and of their long trek up through Mexico to el Norte, the North. The movie represented a breakthrough because it was the first to portray the experience of immigration from the refugees' point of view. Film critic Roger Ebert praised *El Norte* as "one of the rare films that grants Latin Americans full humanity."

The Economic Impact

The Central American community has affected the economic as well as the creative life of the United States, especially in Southern California. The presence of a large Central American population in Southern California has led to vociferous debate on the economic impact of the newcomers. Some believe that Salvadorans, Guatemalans, and Nicaraguans place a large burden on city, county, and state finances because they use public resources, such as the school system, without paying taxes. However, most studies indicate that undocumented immigrants contribute more to the economy than they receive. One examination found that the estimated 1.1 million undocumented Central American immigrants in Los Angeles County added $3 billion in funds to local, state, and federal taxes while using only $213.8 million worth of county services annually—most of that in the schools. Another report concluded that Central Americans receive few public benefits besides medical services because undocumented immigrants rarely qualify for welfare benefits or food stamps.

Complaints about the influx of Central Americans come also from other impoverished ethnic groups who inhabit many of the same districts, including blacks, Mexicans, Koreans, and Vietnamese. Members of these groups accuse Central Americans of appropriating their jobs and aggravating unemployment. But a study prepared by the Urban Institute found that despite recent mass immigration to Southern California, unemployment rates rose less rapidly here than in the rest of the nation, and it cited indications of a continued need for immigrant workers. While they may displace some workers from their jobs, Central Americans create even more jobs both indirectly, through expenditures, and directly, by opening new businesses. Between 1980 and 1986, for example, 500 new Salvadoran-owned businesses opened in southern California.

An Uncertain Future

Although they have succeeded in building a community in the United States, many Central American refugees regard their stay in America as temporary. In one study, Salvadorans were asked under what conditions they would return home. Almost all replied that they would go back if the political situation improved.

"Your president says we are economic refugees," Teresa, a Salvadoran, told the *Sacramento Bee* in August

Looking to a brighter future: Children born to Central Americans living in the United States enter life as U.S. citizens, a first step toward the full participation in American society that has sometimes eluded their parents.

1984. "He says we come to get work. We are only here so we can have the opportunity to live. We hope that peace will come to our country and we can return." Her husband, Oscar, added, "If the revolution is won, we'll be okay. If the Salvadoran military wins, what happens to us? They won't accept us there or here. Where will we go?"

Despite their dream of going home, many Central Americans admit that the possibility of return lies in the distant future. Says one Salvadoran who has been here since 1980, "At the beginning, I thought we would be here maybe two years. I thought, 'Good, my children will learn English.' But now I don't know. I want to go home. My roots are there. But if this situation keeps up, in 10 years there might not be anything to go back to—not even my enemies.''

Not all Central Americans envision a return to their homeland. Those who have prospered in the United States are reluctant to return to the ravaged economy of their native country. Pedro Carlos Melendez and his wife, Clara, came to Houston from El Salvador in 1978 and hope to become U.S. citizens. "Our jobs are on a lower level," Mrs. Melendez told a *New York Times* reporter. "But we have a higher standard of living. We think we can give our children a better education and upbringing than we could there."

The longer families stay in America, the more difficulty they have returning. Children who were born in the United States identify themselves as American and feel little connection with the homeland that calls so strongly to their parents. The greatest hope many families have is that Congress will grant them extended voluntary departure status, thus allowing them to stay here and work until the violence at home subsides.

What the future holds for Central America is uncertain, but it is likely that as long as the violence continues, Central American refugees will feel that they have no choice but to remain in the United States. Many have short-term plans to get a job or a better job, to study English and further their education, and to become involved in self-help groups. They continue to worry about the precarious fate of friends and family back home and to dream about the day they will once again be united. Many share the feelings of a Kanjobal Indian who came in 1974 intending to stay one year but who never returned home: "My heart, my ideas, my imagination are always in my country, my *pueblo*. Someday I will return."

LINCOLN SCHOOL

FURTHER READING

American Civil Liberties Union Foundation. "Salvadorans in the United States: The Case for Extended Voluntary Departure." Washington, DC: Political Asylum Project of the American Civil Liberties Union Fund of the National Capital Area, 1983.

American Friends Service Committee. "In the Shadow of Liberty: Central American Refugees in the United States." Philadelphia: American Friends Service Committee, 1988.

Barry, Tom, and Deb Preusch. *The Central America Fact Book.* New York: Grove Press, 1986.

Booth, John A., and Thomas W. Walker. *Understanding Central America.* Boulder, CO: Westview, 1986.

Cheney, Glenn Alan. *Revolution in Central America.* New York: Watts, 1984.

Cummings, Judith. "The World of the Immigrant: Low-Paying Jobs and Overcrowded Housing." *New York Times,* April 13, 1987.

Ferris, Elizabeth G. *The Central America Refugees.* New York: Praeger, 1986.

Kirk, John M., and George W. Schuyler, eds. *Central America: Democracy, Development and Change.* New York: Praeger, 1988.

LeMoyne, James. "Salvadorans Stream into U.S., Fleeing Poverty and Civil War." *New York Times,* April 13, 1987.

National Public Radio. *Voices in Exile—North of the Border* (tape recording). Washington, DC: National Public Radio, 1987.

Pimlott, John. *South and Central America.* New York: Watts, 1988.

Reimers, David M. *Still the Golden Door: The Third World Comes to America.* New York: Columbia University Press, 1985.

Woo, Elaine. "Inner-City Schools: A Latin Flavor." *Los Angeles Times,* June 25, 1987.

INDEX

PICTURE CREDITS

AP/Wide World Photos: pp. 29, 33, 34, 37, 40–41, 44, 50–51, 55, 58, 62, 92; Marty Baldessari: p. 71; City of Miami/Van Woods: pp. 63, 74; Theodore De Bry, *America:* pp. 25, 27; Mary Kate Denny: pp. 69, 78; El Rescate: pp. 82–83, 91; Tony Freeman/Photo Edit: p. 67; Library of Congress: pp. 28, 31, 32; Felicia Martinez/Photo Edit: pp. 68 (top), 70, 73, 87, 96; M. Richard/Photo Edit: p. 72; Rick Reinhard: cover, pp. 12, 52, 57, 60–61, 65, 66, 68 (bottom), 77, 80, 81, 85, 88, 94, 98–99, 100, 103; Gary Tong: p. 20; United Nations: pp. 15, 16, 18–19, 21, 23, 24, 39, 47, 48, 53; United States Air Force: p. 45

FAREN BACHELIS is a writer of nonfiction books for young adults. She studied anthropology at the University of California at Los Angeles, specializing in Mesoamerican and South American cultures.

DANIEL PATRICK MOYNIHAN is the senior United States senator from New York. He is also the only person in American history to serve in the cabinets or subcabinets of four successive presidents— Kennedy, Johnson, Nixon, and Ford. Formerly a professor of government at Harvard University, he has written and edited many books, including *Beyond the Melting Pot, Ethnicity: Theory and Experience* (both with Nathan Glazer), *Loyalties,* and *Family and Nation.*